THE PUBLIC INTEREST, PORNOGRAPHY, & THE FCC LEADERSHIP DYNAMIC

DR. J. ANTHONY SNORGRASS, PHD

iUniverse, Inc.
Bloomington

The Public Interest, Pornography, &
the FCC Leadership Dynamic

iUniverse books may be ordered through booksellers or by contacting:

iUniverse
1663 Liberty Drive
Bloomington, IN 47403
www.iuniverse.com
1-800-Authors (1-800-288-4677)

ISBN: 978-1-4759-3896-8 (sc)
ISBN: 978-1-4759-3897-5 (ebk)

Printed in the United States of America

iUniverse rev. date: 08/10/2012

Contents

Prologue

Much of the FCC citizen input, participation opportunities, and systems are laced with the values, morality, and social fabric of previous generations, responding poorly to the rapid pace of technology and public demands. This is reflected in the FCC practices impacting citizen involvement, the regulation of communications (including the news media, the press, and television programming), the promotion of public-service advertising (PSAs), and shepherding publicly owned media products. The book examines the legal, political, and social implications of continuing the practice of allowing broadcasters' self-monitored Public Service Broadcasting to satisfy the requirement that radio and television broadcasters serve the public interest. Additionally, the book identifies best practices and benchmarks leading to recommendations intended to improve public-service delivery in support of local community and youth concerns.

American broadcast-media policy has been on a pendulum between liberalization and more restrictive regulation since passage of the 1934 Communications Act, which introduced the Fairness Doctrine as a bridge between pubic interest and commercial interest and vetted regulatory authority with a seven-person Federal Communications Commission (FCC). This pendulum-like sway between deregulation and more restrictive government control has been fueled by advances in technology; shifts in the political, ideological, and moral landscape; and by the distrust of government among many U.S. Americans. Traditional leadership theories provide a historic context for the examination of the leadership role of the legislatively titled (although politically insensitive) FCC chairman in the face of the incessant pressures for media expansion, the introduction of new multi-channel media delivery systems and the explosion of electronic communication alternatives like satellite and wireless transmission, internet, video games, email, instant messaging, e-zines, and text messaging (Hausman, 1999).

The FCC is directed by five Commissioners appointed by the President and confirmed by the Senate for 5-year terms. The President designates one of the Commissioners to serve as Chairperson and only three Commissioners may be members of the same political party (FCC, 2007). There have been 27 individuals to serve as FCC Chairman, some serving more than one term, but there has not been a female to chair the FCC since its inception (FCC, 2007). This places a premium on the leadership the chairman must employ in balancing commercial interests, political interests, and those of the citizenry. Today's highly charged environment focuses on the commercial push for relaxed media-ownership rules, consolidation across mediums, the emergence of user-generated media, and the preponderance of attention being directed toward obscenity, indecency, and profanity across media. Thus the environment threatens this delicate balance and may result in change to the basic tenets of the regulatory scheme established in the 1934 Communications Act which was preceded by the 1927 Federal Radio Act. They established that balance in exchange for free and exclusive use of the publicly owned electromagnetic spectrum of channels, and the premise that broadcasters serve "the public interest, convenience, and necessity" (FCC, 2007). This book focuses on an examination of the organizational dynamics and leadership exhibited by internet-era FCC chairmen in the exercise of their powers in the context of traditional, contemporary and emerging organizational-leadership theories. This is particularly salient with regard to the FCC chairmanship responsibilities in guiding the FCC to determine and protect a fluent public interest and to formulate effective public policy to protect the public airways.

The book will also highlight the FCC's responses to legislative changes, enforcement mechanisms, and policy shifts that reflect its underlying values, assumptions, and leadership dynamics over time. A critical examination will ensue of the historical overview of the FCC organizational structure and chairman's leadership styles and their influence upon legislative initiatives; FCC actions and policy positions impacting e-government; FCC debates and positions regarding free-speech considerations; and FCC stands in safeguarding pubic broadcast spectrums.

Introduction

Given the volatile nature of the challenges that have been placed before the FCC for disposition without any clear and definitive guidelines, the agency has necessarily found some degree of solace in employing an ad hoc and incremental decision-making style (Toth, 1994). Commission decisions have been fraught with reversals from the courts, delays from shifts in internal policy, and a long-standing backlog of claims that renders many actions mute by the time they are taken. Prior to the current push for deregulation, the FCC relied on a detailed and complex system of technical and operational rules that stipulated Broadcaster responsibilities associated with local needs and serving the public interest under what was called the Ascertainment Policy (Napoli, 2006). Grappling with defining the public interest and articulating steps the agency will take to address it have preoccupied much of the strategic energy of the agency at large and its chairman, who often carries the platform. The commission has repeatedly been forced by the courts to redefine how it uses the public-interest standard and fold it into the specific requirements being imposed upon broadcasters from conceptual, operational, and application levels (Napoli, 2006). Broadcasters, to maintain their licenses, must provide programming responsive to community needs; provide a minimum of 3 hours per week of educational and information programs for children; not transmit any obscene, indecent, or profane language; disclose any sponsors of broadcast content; provide reasonable access to legally qualified candidates for federal elected office; provide an opportunity for those having different viewpoints from the broadcasters to air their views; provide some closed captioning; and locate their main studio in a principle signal contour (Napoli, 2006). Even within this allegory of rules, the FCC currently relies on market dynamics driven by consumer demand to guide programming offerings for viewers and listeners that reflect their belief that commercial competition is preferable to behavior-based regulation of broadcasting (Parkinson & Parkinson, 2006).

While the FCC regularity framework focused primarily on the protection of commercial markets, the promotion of universal service and improving access in remote areas arose during the time Charles D. Ferris was chairman between 1977 and 1981. Following this period, the FCC embraced a stronger emphasis on "market force operations" and initiated the practice of licensing new stations to counteract the social- and behavioral-based platforms entertained during the Ferris years (Gilroy, 2004). Chairman Mark Fowler's tenure between 1981and 1987 further reinforced the marketplace model even more fervently than did Ferris. Yet, despite the support for free-market dynamics, the Scarcity Rationale, which is premised on the assumption of a limited electromagnetic spectrum, remained the primary legal and policy argument for government regulation over all electronic media (Parkinson & Parkinson, 2006).

On one hand the broadcast industry insists that they are being treated unfairly under the licensing procedures because First Amendment protections are not extended to them through the limitations included in the licensing agreements. Critics argue that entry thresholds—either through "natural monopoly" or restricting the license availability—effectively advantages broadcasters as the government powers are being used to ration access and involvement in telecommunications businesses. This fuels the classic tension between creating a competitive marketplace out of a monopoly-provided service (Aufderheide, 2000). Breyer and Stewart noted that,

> FCC Commissions operate in hostile environments, and their regulatory policies become conditional upon the acceptance of regulation by the regulated groups. In the long run, a commission is forced to come to terms with the regulated groups as a condition of survival. (Breyer & Stewart, 1979)

Procompetitive critics insist the FCC has become victim to excitement about new communication advances and as as well succumbed to client politics as it has been co-opted by the very industries it was created to regulate (Aufderheide, 2000).

Chapter 1

Encircled by Conflict and Burgeoning with Hysteria

Organizational effectiveness is often measured by the paradoxical balance indicating how well an organization addresses its varied constituencies. Multiple stakeholders increasingly require entities to provide solid evidence of organizational efforts. Productivity is viewed parochially and many times runs counter to the credo of "doing the right things the right way," balancing ethics and effectiveness. Historically, Federal Communications Commission (FCC) leadership has been challenged to use finite human, technological, and financial resources to address priorities of Congress, the White House, other government agencies, legislators, the courts, the media, broadcast-communications industry representatives and lobbies, and individual citizens, as well as the not easily defined "public interest" lumped under the Fairness Doctrine (Crane, 1983). The reality is that U. S. communication policy had historically operated under several laws that had coexisted without clear reconciliation of the ideological positions that prescribed who was to be governed and what role the government should play (Aufderheide, 1999). Innovation and creativity were not the primary objectives of the Communications Act of 1934 as it represented a fusion of mostly laws that had already taken effect (Sussman, 1997). As such, the different directions, cross purposing and tension between these different laws impeded implementation and did not create a clear zone of responsibility for the social effects of the communication processes it had put into motion (Aufderheide).

The FCC leadership and operational quandary was further complicated when the Telecommunications Act of 1996 became law although it was intended to overcome the omissions created by many of the Communications Act of 1934 which had grown obsolete in the new digital environment (Lehman & Weisman, 2000). When President Clinton signed into law the Telecommunications Act of 1996 it signaled an updated, reinforced, clarified, and expanded FCC role in the regulation of the internet, wireless, video, and satellite communications including digital television and a mechanism to respond to any future emerging technologies. The Communications Act of 1934 integrated provisions that would open competition in the regulated industries and spell an end to regulated natural monopolies (Lehman & Weisman).

Yet organizational theory has revealed that complex organizations like the FCC must be viewed in terms of their ability to fulfill their purpose with maximum efficiency (scientific theory); its ability to coordinate and control its intricate levels of authority (bureaucratic and administrative-management theory); the social systems and networks within which employees satisfy their needs (human relations, human resources, and natural-systems theory); the ability to manage uncertainty (open-systems theory); and the symbiotic energy emanating from the unity of shared cultural values and beliefs (organizational-culture theory) (Tompkins,

2005). In this light, each of the aforementioned theoretical foundations calls for the examination of different sets of variables that all influence organizational effectiveness: structural, human, strategic, and symbolic (Tompkins). Focusing on any one of these dynamics and ignoring the others would provide an unreliable foundation on which to comprehend organizational dynamics and provide flawed platforms on which to recommend organizational improvements. Further, it is important to not only review ways to enhance organizational effectiveness, but also to sustain it over time. As such, the focus of this book is to provide a holistic understanding of the structural, leadership, and stakeholder behaviors that serve to shape the context in which the FCC operates.

Chapter 2

Requisites for Effective Public-Interest Stewardship

As an independent regulatory agency the FCC reporting directly to Congress is charged with responsibility over interstate and international communications by radio, television, wire, satellite, and cable throughout each state, the District of Columbia and other United States Possessions (Hilliard, 1991). Only congressional legislation and federal court decisions may alter or approve, abolish, or uphold FCC responsibilities and authority (Hilliard). The FCC derives its fundamental powers to regulate the broadcast and communications industries through the Communications Act of 1934, promulgated to consolidate the government's role in regulating disparate regulations spread across many government agencies including the Federal Radio Commission, the Department of Commerce, and the Interstate Commerce Commission (Sterling & Kittross, 2002).

President Franklin D. Roosevelt appointed an interdepartmental committee to examine the roles of these agencies involved with public, private, and governmental use of radio, which envisioned and recommended the creation of the FCC under a broad and nonrestrictive legislative mandate to assure its utmost flexibility (Sterling & Kittross, 2002). The FCC was created as a result of this initiative as an independent federal agency under the Communications Act of 1934 (Title 47 of the United States Code). Section 1 of the Act states,

> For the purpose of regulating interstate and foreign commerce in communication by wire and radio so as to make available, so far as possible, to all the people of the United States, without discrimination on the basis of race, color, religion, national origin, or sex, a rapid, efficient, Nation-wide, and world-wide wire and radio communication service with adequate facilities at reasonable charges, for the purpose of the national defense, for the purpose of promoting safety of life and property through the use of wire and radio communications, and for the purpose of securing a more effective execution of this policy by centralizing authority heretofore granted by law to several agencies and by granting additional authority with respect to interstate and foreign commerce in wire and radio communication, there is created a commission to be known as the "Federal Communications Commission", which shall be constituted as hereinafter provided, and which shall execute and enforce the provisions of this chapter (Hilliard, 1991).

The intent was to create extremely broad policy parameters and authoritative latitude for the FCC over all interstate radio, line, and wire communications, with the specific intent of making an efficient communications service available to all people (Hilliard, 1991). These broad policy parameters were justified given the recognition that ever-evolving media technology impacting radio broadcasting, and expanding telecommunication content (the convergence of news, entertainment, persuasion, and culture), process (medium of transmission), and format (physical form of information) required different approaches from those necessary previously (Compaine, 1984).

The rapid pace of technological change introducing television, cable and satellite, cell phones, and wireless computing prompted many amendments to the 1934 Communications Act (Lehman & Weisman, 2000). Chief among them was the Communications Satellite Act of 1962 and the Cable Act of 1992 which vested expanded authorities and regulatory oversight responsibilities with the FCC (Wilson, 2000). But the initial arc of policy and operational flexibility incorporated into the general provisions of the Communications Act of 1934 has allowed the FCC to respond to many of the new technology and consumer trends and establish a policy and regulatory framework (Sussman, 1997).

The primary impetus for such broad reaching legislative authority was born out of the controversy associated with the allocation of frequencies to radio stations (Vivian, 2006). The 1927 FRC was given authorization to license radio frequency use, but the system was already overloaded as 732 stations had been authorized to broadcast despite the fact that the technology of the time only supported use by 568 stations (Vivian). The FRC's response was to impose a licensure process assigning frequencies to stations for limited, although renewable, terms that it hoped would mitigate the conflicts and prevent signal over-lap (Vivian). The FRC, using its premise that radio is a public domain that must be operated in the fullest and highest interests of the public, instituted a process in which each and every license had to be reviewed every 3 years (Heffron, 1983). The result was the achievement of silencing many stations and the opening of a long-standing dialogue concerning the government's role in regulating mediums that purveyed information and ideas to citizens (Wilson, 2000). Although the FRC was able to establish important technical, procedural, and legal precedents, many felt that the government's entry into this form of regulation was a direct First Amendment violation (Weinberg, 1983). In this sense the airwaves were established as public property and should be subject to regulation as a public good in much the same manner as public roads, water, and electricity (Haigh, Gerber, & Byrne, 1981). Further, the 1927 Federal Radio Act established the threshold measure for granting licenses only to those stations that could clearly establish that their use served "public interest, convenience, and necessity" (Vivian, 2006). Similarly, the Federal government had clearly established its "trustee" interest in airway transmission that would extend into the imposition of technological requirements that limit station power and facilitate squeezing more stations onto a single frequency; ownership controls intended to prevent big media chains from monopolizing frequencies and encourage diversity of ownership; and content considerations to assure broadcast decency in line with prevailing morals (Vivian). These concepts were introduced in the provisions of the Federal Communications Act of 1934 and reinforced through subsequent reform of the Telecommunications Act in 1996 (Crandall, 2007).

Despite the many amendments, both Congress and the FCC have maintained broad oversight over all broadcasting regulations and have historically viewed their role as a referee among various competing technologies for scarce resources (Haigh et al., 1981). Although the FCC uses an auctioning system to determine who would be awarded licenses to provide consumer services, it then enforces public policy through the imposition of rules, regulations, and requirements to retain licensure standing. Major issues are brought before the full commission at regular monthly meetings while more parochial policy-setting matters are assigned to individual commissioners for resolution (Hilliard, 1991).

The language of the 1934 Communications Act and 1996 Telecommunications Act were written sufficiently broad to serve as a flexible foundation to promulgate new rules and regulations targeting the ever-changing array of emergent digital services and electronic technologies. However, the FCC must operate under the watchful eye of the federal court which in *Quincy Cable TV, Inc. v. FCC*, admonished the FCC of its responsibility to base its rules only upon substantiated research and study (Furchtgott-Roth, 2006).

As expected, there has always been strong resistance to the FCC's regulatory authority by the broadcast industry which had previously only been subject to self-regulation through the National Association of Broadcasters and other media-specific trade organizations. That independent stance provided a precursor to the constant battles that have ensued throughout the FCC's existence (Sterling & Kittross, 2002). Although the 1934 Federal Communications Act expressly forbid censorship and provisions in the the 1996 Telecommunications Act of was absent language supporting censorship, the focus of the FCC has included a strong program clean-up emphasis in which the FCC intended to change what was considered to be substandard programming and advertising policies by determining whether individual station operations, policies and programming existed within the public interests through its licensure renewal process for radio-frequency assignments (Sterling & Kittross). Supported by the 1934 legislation, the FCC also was to bolster investigations of monopolies particularly in the telephone industry, reduce lobbying activity of broadcasters to influence Congress, dissolve the concentration of ownership of broadcast systems, and implement the fairness doctrine which was intended to assure the airing of myriad viewpoints (Sterling & Kittross).

Chapter 3

Coddling the Power and Raft of Congress

The FCC operates from a position of strength that is experienced by only a select few agencies in that it possesses the combined powers of all branches of government. Legislative, executive, and judicial powers were vested with it when it was created in 1934 (Furchtgott-Roth, 2005). Unlike many other federal agencies with a direct public interest responsibility, the FCC chair does not hold a position on the President's cabinet as the agency is "independent" agency of any obligation to work with other federal agencies (Hilliard, 1991). Further, the FCC chairman nor its member's terms are subject to the will of the President (Cannon, 2000). Instead, as an adjudicative and administrative agency, legislatively the U.S. Congress is the only entity to which the FCC is answerable (Wilson, 2000).

The FCC is overseen by the Commerce Committees of the House and Senate. The Senate Commerce, Science and Transportation Committee is chaired by Senator Daniel K. Inouye (D-HI) known for his reputation as a legislative leader on maritime and communication policy. The House Committee on Energy and Commerce is chaired by Representative John Dingell (D-MI). These committees exercise tremendous influence affecting communications policy and regularly hold hearings on a wide range of direct and tangentially related issues including telecommunication company mergers, internet gambling, the deployment of high speed internet, and the safety of children on the internet (Cannon, 2000).

Due to this organizational ambiguity, autonomy, and independence, Furchtgott-Roth, a former FCC Commission chairman, postulated that Congress, other government branches, the broadcasters, nor the citizenry will ever be entirely satisfied with FCC actions (Furchtgott-Roth, 2005). Furchtgott-Roth furthers insisted that this concentration of power allows the FCC to write its own rules, enforce them as it sees fit, and adjudicate disputes under them, leading to considerable inefficiency in its operations and ultimately contributing to what has been perceived as an arrogance of nonresponsiveness to the public will and popular politics (Furchtgott-Roth). As a result, the FCC has historically had little incentive to seek precision in rulemaking, clarity, certainty, and nondiscrimination in either its administration or adjudication (Furchtgott-Roth). Others have argued that this autonomy has fostered an environment that has become self-perpetuating, anti-innovation, and oblivious to the potential benefits of strategic and organizational planning that may enhance effectiveness.

Organizationally, the FCC is comprised of seven separate branches and divisions. The broadcaster licensing and regulation is the primary responsibility of the Mass Media Bureau and as such this entity is often the most publicly visible component of the agency. Implementation of the provisions of the Cable Act of 1992 affecting interstate communications service providers primarily rest with the

Common Carrier Bureau while the Private Radio Bureau regulates the full set of microwave, mobile, and satellite communication services. Most public outreach programs, enforcement actions, and engineering services are handled by this unit and it has the widest opportunity for direct public contact. Most of the compliance testing and equipment checks for FCC compliance are performed by the Office of Engineering and Technology (FCC, 1999).

The former Office of Plans and Policy has been replaced by the Office of Strategic and Policy Analysis (OSP) which is responsible for the state of the communications industry and trend monitoring overall industry health (FCC, 1999). The OSP is responsible for developing a strategic plan identifying short-term and long-term policy objectives for the agency. The OSP also serves as an internal expert consultant producing economic, business, and market analysis, which cut across traditional lines like the Internet, intellectual property law, and e-commerce issues (FCC, 1999).

The first commission members were Eugene O. Sykes, Thad H. Brown, Paul A. Walker, Norman Case, Irvin Stewart, George Henry Paine, and Hampson Gary. All possessed backgrounds in administration or law, or represented regulated industries (Hilliard, 1991).

Chapter 4

Policy Ambivalence
and the Public's Interest

Policy is decided at the FCC by simple vote of the five commissioners (Cannon, 2000). Generally commission business is conducted in meetings that are open to the public and broadcast via C-SPAN and over the internet. Most matters are brought before the FCC, through the FCC bureau docket, and where appropriate a vote may be called for and taken (Cannon). A simple majority rule applies to all decisions of the commission. However, as a matter of public record, dissenting commissioners have the opportunity and often attach dissenting opinions to the decisions of the FCC (Aufderheide, 1999).

Serving citizens, thinking democratically, and protecting the "ill-defined" public interest are laudable pursuits, but they often couch FCC initiatives so that they are viewed as direct violations of the First Amendment and thus invite administrative and legal challenges. Despite this exposure, the FCC has taken stern positions and imposed hefty penalties for violations by the companies it regulates. The FCC position resembles George Savile's theory on deterrence articulated by the 17th century Marquis of Halifax, "Men are not hanged for stealing horses, but that horses may not be stolen" (Denhardt, Denhardt, & Aristigueta, 2002). In accord with this preventive-based strategy, FCC violators are not penalized harshly for merely the actual infringements, but so that future violations will not occur. The FCC has historically maintained a no-nonsense policy in assuring that radio and television licensees maintain good character and that they follow accepted business practices aimed towards the achievement of the letter, intent and spirit of applicable laws and FCC regulations. This was evidenced by its 1969 revocation of the Jackson, Mississippi WLB-TV license because it made no attempt to hire Blacks even though Jackson was a predominately Black community (Vivian, 2006). The levying and enforcement of fines has proven to be a controversial activity for the FCC as many broadcasters who have faced violations based on claims that they aired obscene and indecent incidents have lambasted the FCC for not issuing clear and definitive guidance in this area. In 1991, the FCC fined a St. Louis station, KSHE, $25,000 after a disc jockey broadcast a mock nuclear attack on the United States (Ahrens, 2005). Similarly, a Los Angeles church-owned radio station license was revoked after its preacher blasphemed Jews, lawyers, judges, and others on the air (Ahrens). After winning a Supreme Court ruling supporting its ruling of George Carlin's seven dirty words as indecent in 1975, the FCC imposed a $1.3 million fine on Howard Stern and Infinity Broadcasting (Ahrens). Recently, the FCC has stepped up pressure on broadcasters to diminish sexual content following the Janet Jackson "wardrobe malfunction" and Bono's use of vulgar language during live broadcasts. In an effort to both discourage and protect broadcasters from impugning themselves, the FCC has imposed a 5-second delay on most live broadcasts and has requested a "safe harbor" for programming of a mature and questionable content to a broadcasting window between 10:00 P.M. and 6:00 A.M. (Greppi, Halonen, & Lisotta, 2005).

Despite these actions, many community-interest proponents are openly critical of the FCC's argument that its initiatives supporting convergence and deregulation have essentially served the needs of large broadcast interests (McChesney & Schiller, 2002). Community advocates have viewed early FCC proceedings as revealing a pattern of disfavoring educational or community interests against business and commercial interests in license proceedings (Greppi et al., 2005). On the other hand, major broadcast interests argue that historically FCC actions have worked against commercial media interests by imposing rules prohibiting firms from owning Television stations and newspapers in the same communities and limiting the number of cable and television stations any one company can own nationally (McChesney & Schiller, 2002).

Most recently FCC attention has been directed toward the priority for emergency services, alerts, communication infrastructure alerts, and disaster management (Napoli, 2001). Regulations affecting the public security and safety, is being pursued in the interest of addressing the need for immediate communication solutions in response to breakdowns experienced during 9/11 tragedy responses (Guttman-McCabe and Mushahwar, 2005). This initiative is premised on strengthening homeland security rather than protection of individual First Amendment considerations. The industry has shifted toward greater business involvement in framing regulations through "private—public partnerships" evidenced by the prioritization of the Critical Infrastructure Information Act, Outage Reporting, and the Wireless Priority Service, (Guttman-McCabe and Mushahwar).

Chapter 5

The Roots of Regulatory Dysfunction

Although the FCC is considered a part of the executive branch it is actually a regulatory agency and its administrative head is not a Presidential cabinet member the position does require nomination by the President and confirmation by the Senate prior to appointment (Hilliard, 1991). Despite this appointment authority given to Presidents, a sitting political party is only permitted a majority of one which means that any sitting President can appoint no more than three members (Hilliard). The original 1934 Communications Act called for the FCC to be comprised of seven members, although membership was reduced to five in 1983. The President's power to designate one member to serve as chairman often imposes a political debt to the person who appointed them (Hilliard). The power and influence of the chairman is no more obvious than in the recognition that the chairman has the authority to appoint all bureau and department heads at its discretion and in this sense sets the overall agency agenda and functioning.

In this light, it is not surprising that the FCC reflects the ideology of the political party that occupies the White House and the often patronage-driven leadership of the chairman.

According to Robert Taylor and William E. Rosenbach, "Leadership is . . . an elusive and hazy concept. There are almost as many definitions of leadership as there are people attempting to define it" (Taylor & Rosenbach, 2001). With regard to the FCC, leadership must be defined as it relates to the process by which constituent groups and appointed leaders engage in reciprocal influence to achieve stated organizational purposes.

Applying the principles of open-systems theory suggests that organizations like the FCC should be viewed as adaptive systems that must continually interact with their environment and as totally dependent on successful interactions with their environment for survival (Katz & Kahn 1978). Most challenges for the FCC are expectantly multidimensional in scope. The solutions, then, require a complexity that is only addressed by an interdisciplinary team approach where individuals are expected to bring their respective knowledge, expertise, and requisite skills forming a unified attack to the problem-solving effort. Heffron suggested that the FCC is best viewed as an open system in that its primary role has been to seek equilibrium or a stable state wherein those constituent interest bearers in the environment who seek change are counterbalanced by those who desire either no change or a change in the opposite direction (Heffron, 1983). According to Heffron, the success of the FCC and its ability to survive can be measured by observing the extent to which it has successfully balanced interactions with its varied stakeholders—lobbying groups, other agencies, trade organizations, and individuals (Heffron). The FCC's environment constantly engages the often-conflicting political, technological, legal, economic, cultural, demographic, and ecological dimensions that serve to intensify the degree of turbulence as well as diminish the opportunity to maintain a productive equilibrium (Moon, 1999). Under the auspices of the chairman, FCC responses have ranged form using the tools of charisma and inspirational leadership to manage conflicts and balance interests; consensus building to decrease the parochialism of interest groups; and administrative skills aimed at developing structure and formalizing relationships between stakeholders—all in an attempt to diminish the complexity of the challenges (Heffron).

Largely in response to these dynamics, many FCC Commissioners who have appeared to possess all of the requisite technical skills, interpersonal, and management qualities suggestive of effective leadership haven't necessarily succeeded in managing the FCC's entrenchment with conflict. And where some have succeeded, their efforts often are considered to have resulted in great harm or tragedy to citizen rights and society at large. Characterizing and understanding the varied leadership of FCC commissioners requires the overlay of some classical leadership theories including the great-man theory where leaders are portrayed as heroic and Herculean; trait theories which insist that leaders possess inherent qualities and traits that position them for leadership positions; contingency theory in which leadership responses are determined by the variables presented by certain situations; participative theories where designated leaders take others' positions into account in the decision-making process; and transformational theories which focus upon the relationships between leaders and followers that serve as motivation and inspiration to move an organization toward exceptional performance (Bolden, Gosling, Marturano, & Dennison, 2003).

Historically, FCC chairmen have displayed diverse styles including many of the leadership characteristics modeled in these theories but most have been successful in using "issue enlightenment and symbolism platforms" as a means of attracting media and public awareness to problems in broadcasting needing redress. Considered the most famous and controversial chairman, Newton Minow (1961-1963) referred to television as "a vast wasteland" in an effort to challenge broadcasters to raise programming standards (Shales, 2004). Richard Wiley, who was chairman between 1972 and 1977 took sharp aim at the issues related to children's television and the adverse impact of advertising practices directed toward them (Messere, 2002). Mark Fowler (1981-1987) made his mark by proclaiming that "television is just another appliance . . . a toaster with pictures" as he pushed for broadcasters to be viewed less as trustees of the public interest and more as a business interest (Potter, 2003). Alfred Sikes (1989-1992) has been highly recognized as the commission chairman who called on the agency to strive for "a renewed commitment to the public trust," built on his criticism of the degree of television news coverage and commercial time broadcast during children's programming. His actions led to the initiation of a detailed FCC evaluation of individual station practices with regard to programming for children at license renewal (Williams, 1993).

Symbolically, especially in learning organizations, leadership is often viewed as art while management is viewed as science (Senge & Kleiner, 1999). The leadership challenge is to craft a shared vision while assuring the institutionalization of a management structure to achieve that vision (Shafritz, Ott, & Jang, 2005). But, in the context of organizational performance and achievement, these distinctions often morph into each other and create a very complex web of shared components and attributes (Senge & Kleiner). The FCC quagmire is even more complex as the dynamic relationship between leadership and management are overlaid with the nuances of public interest, government bureaucracy, politics, and operational responsibilities. The challenge of sustaining momentum in learning organizations rest primarily with the leadership, charged with creating a strategic vision and management system that delivers policy and programs through a well-sequenced path of orchestrated activities (Tompkins, 2005).

According to Frederick Taylor's theory, leader effectiveness in achieving organizational outcomes rests on the leader's talents in motivating workers (Tompkins, 2005). Others feel that this level of influence is achieved primarily because of a leader's wealth, military might, or position (Bolden et al., 2003). Newton Minow readily admitted that his appointment was solely because he was a collegiate roommate of President Kennedy (Weinberg, 1983). Other FCC Chairmen were selected because they possessed superior legal, technical, or political acumen. There are others who were appointed because of who they knew or who happened to rise into leadership because of unique circumstances (Acumen, 2003). This vertical-dyad linkage model of leadership opportunity suggests that the most successful leadership style is chameleon-like in order to meet the relationship dynamics that may change with each individual circumstance confronting the FCC.

FCC commissioners' duties include the delegation of work matters to appropriate bureaus, staff and committees as well as the supervision of supervise all FCC activities. In this sense, FCC leadership is a complex moral relationship based on obligation, commitment, trust, strong emotions, and a shared vision of good similar to that exhibited in the arena of sports team leaders (Acumen, 2003). As such, the FCC chairmanship is akin to stewardship. Stewardship is premised on choosing service over self-interest and emphasizes a total redistribution of the traditional trappings of leadership. Under stewardship, control and consistency is replaced with partnerships and choice at all levels. Leaders who envision themselves as stewards internalize responsibility over entitlement and challenge themselves to act with sincere accountability to subordinates; and forthrightly address issues of ethics and trust (Block, 1993).

According to Bolden, the best leaders are felt to be those who work effectively in internal and external dominions of leadership (Bolden et al., 2003). Leadership, while based upon the exercise of power, primarily rests upon formal authority bestowed by a higher authority, and for the FCC that power is vested through the Congress. In this sense, organizational effectiveness is beholden to a sense of legitimacy that comes from the legal or perceived authority bestowed by some higher social institution. FCC leadership, though, bears no such burden because it represents a willing exchange based on the currency of perceived expertise, reference, reward, rights, or coercion to assure conformance (Parkinson & Parkinson, 2006). FCC leadership may be more temporal than that of other regulatory agencies in that it relies more heavily on the ability of the leader to quickly establish a complimentary organizational culture, and certain leadership styles lose effectiveness as moral positions and political ideologies change over time (Pearce, 2004). This is especially salient given the limited terms FCC commissioners are allowed to serve.

Although it assures a dominant political-party influence, undue pressure from the executive branch and a bipartisan atmosphere is maintained because each commissioner may only serve for a period of 5 years, and it is unlawful for a sitting President to appoint to the commission more than three members of any one political party. A significant body of leadership research has been devoted to identifying the ideal approach for FCC leaders, yet no single style or personality has proven sustainable across situations. However, it has become increasingly clear that the FCC chairman, acting alone, can often achieve significant policy movement. But the more tenuous, uncertain and complex the policy spectrum, the participative style is considered to have greater potential for success. Participatory decision-making, however, is quite time consuming because the path to consensus is often long and tedious, resulting in considerable public criticism of the FCC for allowing policy dockets to remain open for extended time periods, creating the appearance of inaction (Linker, 1983). Thus timing and task orientation appear to be equally essential to successful leadership in the FCC. When decisions must be made quickly, the chairman must act alone on available information and, very often, on intuition (Taylor & Rosenbach, 1998). This certainly describes the saga of Michael Powell's tenure as chairman.

Chairman Michael Powell presented his platform as a moderate Republican advancing a plan to heighten the internal expertise and technological acumen and to overhaul the agency's organizational structure to reflect market realities, and establish a clear policy vision for the FCC (Fisher, 2002). Powell felt that the FCC had become ineffective in addressing its mission because of the duplicity of multiple bureaus addressing the same competitive environments. Further, he put forth that using the Telecommunications Act of 1996 provisions, he could eliminate the separate mass media, cable, and other industry-specific bureaus and more efficiently organize the FCC around licensing, enforcement, and spectrum management (Fischer). The strategy Powell employed was to consult regularly with Senate and House leadership and to functionally align the agency as the "eyes and ears" for lawmakers, leaving the decision to act or not act to their discretion (Fischer). Powell garnered strong support from the broadcast industry, assuring broadcasters that he would not pressure them to curb what they air in exchange for favorable regulatory treatment by the agency (Fischer). Powell also spoke mockingly of the "imaginary angel of the public interest" as he proclaimed his sacred duty to protect corporate media interests. Powell's leadership style was based on the use of praise and encouragement rather than criticism, although he clearly established that he was in charge and admonished his staff for leaking any information to the press, and ignored or condemned anyone who opposed him (Shales, 2004). However, Powell's top-down management style did not sit well in bringing political or policy compromise among the other commissioners, who were embarrassed by the inaction, and Powell's relinquishment of regulation to Congress under the forbearance doctrine where the FCC could, on its own initiative, choose not to regulate an industry segment.

Fred E. Fiedler's research is recognized as a forerunner in the investigation of contingencies that alter and affect leadership styles and behavior. Fiedler based his theory on the relationships of positional power, the nature of the subordinate's task, and the interpersonal relationship. Instead of focusing on leader personality traits the path—goal or expectancy theory, a cousin to Fiedler's contingent theory, focuses on the situation and leader behavior. It suggests that success will be based directly upon the degree to which behavioral expectations result in desired outcomes, as well as how the value placed upon these outcomes by a leader. This leadership approach befits that employed by Kevin Martin as he ascended to the chairmanship after a 4-year stint on the commission where he was staunch defender of localism and local broadcaster demands for province over contracts with the major networks and for expanded rights to carry select cable offerings in designated digital markets (McConnell, 2005). Relying on President Bush's social-conservative allies, Martin felt that he would be successful in steering the FCC's review of rules affecting broadcast ownership towards relaxing the restriction on the number of stations any one owner can possess in any one market to three and eliminating the ban on cross-ownership of stations and newspapers in the same market (McConnell). Leveraging his strong personal stand against broadcast indecency, Martin's agenda to use hefty fees to discourage broadcasters from violating indecency restrictions, complete the digital-television transition, and settle allegations that the networks have abused their market position over affiliated stations were viewed positively by the then Republican-led Congress (McConnell).

Chapter 6

Reclaiming Public Stewardship through Druckerism

Simply put, the FCC relies upon information as its preferred currency in negotiating the increased layers of vested interest groups. According to Peter Drucker, this value-laden information exchange and distribution qualifies the FCC as an information-based organization (Drucker, 1988). Drucker recognized the power the FCC to strategically use information as a means to maintain political and market equilibrium. He insisted that organizations operating in this manner are "more likely to resemble a hospital or a symphony than a typical manufacturing company" if they are to sustain effectiveness in such a rapidly changing, difficult-to-anticipate environment (Drucker, 1988). Drucker advocated complete specialization, where each organization unit is highly qualified in a particular area in the way x-ray, pharmacy, and surgery all have unique and particular functions although all directed toward the common goal of patient care. In a symphonic venue, each instrument produces a separate sound directed to the performance (Drucker, 1988). With the 1998 publication of "The Coming of the New Organization," Drucker imagined how organizations would appear by 2008. According to Drucker, the 21st century typical organization would be knowledge based and composed largely of specialists (Drucker. 1988). It is this that represents a complete and dynamic contrast from the standard manufacturing orientation of Frederick Herzberg's theories on motivation in the workplace. Drucker, a predecessor of Herzberg's work, is often credited with suggesting the notion that, "What you have to do and the way you have to do it is incredibly simple. Whether you are willing to do it . . . that's another matter (Drucker, 1988). The restructuring of the FCC to become the steward of the public interest is organizationally quite simple, in fact the FCC is already structured to capitalize on the specialization required to achieve this. The challenge is a political one.

These principles of specialization are important as they relate to the concept of rationality as it affects the quality and structure of decision-making and the accomplishment of work efficiency. Simon argued, in his classic, *Administrative Behavior*, that real people cannot handle all the information that is available to make clearly rational decisions using the economic-man model, so he introduced the administrative-man model based on a satisficing approach to decision making (Denhardt, 2002). This approach certainly increases the opportunities for effectiveness in decision making because it brings a sense of reality and manageability to the process. This is all the more important, recognizing the process-induced elements of self-interest and its influence on the inconsistencies between organizational goals and individual interests that has also given rise to the organizational-process model and the governmental-politics model. Both of these models recognize a collaborative of loosely allied organizations that have the opportunity to view things from quite different perspectives. The administrative-man model would allow the FCC to cease to consider itself a referee among interest groups and adopt a new framework for policy and its implementation as an instrument of the consuming public, both individual and business (Haigh et al., 1981). This platform would lend a directional platform on which to build to an organizational culture that emerges to shape the behavior of individuals in these organizations and outside of them (Denhardt et al., 2002).

Chapter 7

Porn Industry Out Shadow Boxes FCC
(aka, Porn Access Trumps Universal Access)

Given the volatile nature of the challenges that have been placed before the FCC for disposition without any clear and definitive guidelines, the agency has necessarily found some degree of solace in employing an ad hoc and incremental decision-making style (Toth, 1994). Commission decisions have been fraught with reversals from the courts, delays from shifts in internal policy, and a long-standing backlog of claims that renders many actions mute by the time they are taken. Prior to the current push for deregulation, the FCC relied on a detailed and complex system of technical and operational rules that stipulated Broadcaster responsibilities associated with local needs and serving the public interest under what was called the Ascertainment Policy (Napoli, 2006). Grappling with defining the public interest and articulating steps the agency will take to address it have preoccupied much of the strategic energy of the agency at large and its chairman, who often carries the platform. The commission has repeatedly been forced by the courts to redefine how it uses the public-interest standard and fold it into the specific requirements being imposed upon broadcasters from conceptual, operational, and applicational levels (Napoli, 2006). Broadcasters, to maintain their licenses, must provide programming responsive to community needs; provide a minimum of 3 hours per week of educational and information programs for children; not transmit any obscene, indecent, or profane language; disclose any sponsors of broadcast content; provide reasonable access to legally qualified candidates for federal elected office; provide an opportunity for those having different viewpoints from the broadcasters to air their views; provide some closed captioning; and locate their main studio in a principle signal contour (Napoli, 2006). Even within this allegory of rules, the FCC currently relies on market dynamics driven by consumer demand to guide programming offerings for viewers and listeners that reflect their belief that commercial competition is preferable to behavior-based regulation of broadcasting (Parkinson & Parkinson, 2006).

While the FCC regularity framework focused primarily on the protection of commercial markets, the promotion of universal service and improving access in remote areas arose during the time Charles D. Ferris was chairman between 1977 and 1981. Following this period, the FCC embraced a stronger emphasis on "market force operations" and initiated the practice of licensing new stations to counteract the social- and behavioral-based platforms entertained during the Ferris years (Gilroy, 2004). Chairman Mark Fowler's tenure between 1981and 1987 further reinforced the marketplace model even more fervently than did Ferris. Yet, despite the support for free-market dynamics, the Scarcity Rationale, which is premised on the assumption of a limited electromagnetic spectrum, remained the primary legal and policy argument for government regulation over all electronic media (Parkinson & Parkinson, 2006).

On one hand the broadcast industry insists that they are being treated unfairly under the licensing procedures because First Amendment protections are not extended to them through the limitations included in the licensing agreements. Critics argue that entry thresholds—either through "natural monopoly" or restricting the license availability—effectively advantages broadcasters as the government powers are being used to ration access and involvement in telecommunications businesses. This fuels the classic tension between creating a competitive marketplace out of a monopoly-provided service (Aufderheide, 2000). Breyer and Stewart noted that,

> FCC Commissions operate in hostile environments, and their regulatory policies become conditional upon the acceptance of regulation by the regulated groups. In the long run, a commission is forced to come to terms with the regulated groups as a condition of survival. (Breyer & Stewart, 1979)

Procompetitive critics insist the FCC has become victim to excitement about new communication advances and as as well succumbed to client politics as it has been co-opted by the very industries it was created to regulate (Aufderheide, 2000).

Nowhere has this dynamic been more obvious than FCC Chairman Kevin Martin's push for a free, no-porn wireless Internet network across the USA. Martin's ambitious proposal for the free Internet network was to create a nationwide broadband network for use by all and stave off criticism that under his tenure the US had fallen in international broadband Internet ranking. The proposal also challenged the dominance of the wireless phone market by AT&T, and Verizon plus the much smaller providers like T-Mobile and Sprint by infusing competition via an auction for new Advanced Wireless Services 3 band – 2155-2180MHz) airwaves with the requirement that 1/4th of the spectrum be used for free consumer use with smut filtering. "This initiative brings with it the promise o free basic broadband service to hundreds of thousands of Americans who currently have limited or no access to high-speed Internet, Martin said. "It is important that we find new and creative ways to make broadband services more accessible, reliable and robust throughout our nation and this initiative will help us to meet that goal" (FCC, 2008).

The winners of the auction would be able to charge premium fees for services on the remaining spectrum that could have faster speeds than the free service. The provider would have been required to honor a *Carterfone-style* rule that allows any application or device to connect to the network. According to an Ars Technica 2008 report, the intent was to license the spectrum for 10 years, with unlimited 10 year renewal periods (Lasar, 2008). The Martin dubbed free "lifeline broadband service' on the other hand, would have a filter to keep pornography and other material deemed not suitable for children off the network although adults could opt out of that feature.

Despite the 'close the digital divide' merits of Martin's proposal, strong resistance came from incumbent wireless service providers who were fearful the new network would cause interference to its existing and future users. T-Mobile, a unit of Germany's Deutsche Telecom after spending $4 billion for a nearby spectrum disputed a report from the FCC that rejected the firm's interference claims. Additionally, a plethora of consumer advocacy groups and civil liberties advocates objected to Martin's idea of filtering adult content on the public network often calling it a scheme to support government-sanctioned censorship.

Ars Technia (December 2008) reported that groups like Public Knowledge, Consumers Union, and the Media Access project indicated their support of the basic "free internet" idea but sans filtering and with even more stringent open access requirements (Lasar, 2008). Notwithstanding, the Bush Whitehouse and the Republican Party shared no such promise in the proposal echoing via a letter to Martin from then Secretary of Commerce Carlos Gutierrez that the proposal represented a waste of taxpayers' funds, impeded market place competition, and involved government in markets more fitting for the private sector. However, sensing the proposals eminent doom, Martin in the hopes of marshaling support for a last ditch push before leaving office upon the inauguration of the Obama administration in January 2009, dropped the controversial porn filtering requirement. Despite the offer of compromise, the proposal did not garner sufficient votes from the FCC members to even get on the docket for consideration.

Martin resigned his position as Chair of the FCC on January 20, 2009, the day Barack Obama was inaugurated as President, signaling a *tko* [technical knock-out] over porn filtering and as well, martin's hope for free universal Internet access.

Part II

Conflict and Compromise: the Protestation of the Public Interest Through the The Telecommunications Act of 1996

Chapter 8

The FCC as Disruptive Innovator

The first composite revision to the Communications Act of 1934 was represented by the Telecommunications Act of 1996 (Troy, 2001). It's passage signaled a Congressional commitment to "promote competition and reduce regulation." Many citizen advocates, industry representatives and legislators believed that the 1996 Act would "secure lower prices and higher quality services for American telecommunications consumers and encourage the rapid deployment of new telecommunications technologies" (Aufderheide, 1999). With promises of being the "revolutionary legislation of the Clinton era, the 1996 Act was aimed at bringing technology to the doorsteps of every citizen in the United States (Furchtgott-Roth, 2006).

The1996 Telecommunications Act was intended to overcome "outdated, invasive regulation," which had imposed a heavy financial burden and drain on the public budget. Nonetheless, President Clinton submitted spiraling budget requests for the FCC: a 20% hike in the FCC's budget for fiscal year 2000 and an 11.5% increase for fiscal year 2001 (Troy, 2001). Notwithstanding, the FCC continued to implement and enforce regulations that had become obsolete and the organization refused to yield to pressure from a Republican Congress to unleash U.S. communications markets (Ellig, 2006).

Recognizing the unmitigated pace and perpetual change in the telecommunications industry, today's FCC challenge is to do more with less while assuring that the U.S. public benefits from the explosive changes represented in the competitive, and innovative telecommunications industry envisioned by the Telecommunications Act (Brenner, 2005). To further complicate this task, the proliferation of cable networks and the internet energized an explosion of public interest groups as the FCC continues to come under a barrage of challenges to every policy and decision it makes (Heffron, 1983). Many FCC watchdog organizations including the Accuracy in Media (AIM), Action for Children's Television (ACT), Black Efforts for Soul in Television (BEST), Citizen's Communication Center (CCC), Media Access Project (MAP), National Association for Better Broadcasting, National Black Media Coalition, National Latino Media Coalition, Common Cause, Free Press, and the Center for Media and Democracy—all considered to have a stake in the decisions made by the FCC—have pushed the FCC in often-conflicting directions in an all-out effort to lobby for a prescriptive role in issues of particular and often parochial concern to them. These carry-forward organizational issues include:

- ☐ diminished reliance on the merger review process as a policy platform;
- ☐ reduced regulations;
- ☐ cultivating a customer-centric culture;
- ☐ restricted growth and expansion;
- ☐ abandonment of regulating media content;

- □   modification of ownership restrictions to promote diversity;
- □   abandonment of attempts to regulate the internet; and
- □   restructuring spectrum allocation policies (Bauer & Wildman, 2006).

According to testimony before the Subcommittee on Telecommunications and the Internet Committee on Energy and Commerce, FCC Commissioner McDowell warned that overlaying these structural problems with a plethora of existing and anticipated regulatory challenges of spectrum auctions, public safety interoperability, reviewing broadcast-ownership rules, deployment into spectrum white spaces, release of digital audio broadcasting rules, and extension of video franchising orders to video providers requires the FCC to transcend traditional regulatory paradigms (hrg.031407: Regulatory Philosophy, 2007). McDowell recognized that technological developments were yielding untold opportunities for consumers to improve their quality of life, businesses to improve competitiveness, and as well for the FCC to improve its operational efficiency (McDowell). McDowell challenged the FCC to transition from the legacy regulations that govern individual industries, clear the unnecessary regulatory underbrush, tear down historic entry barriers, and move to a more nimble structure to ensure fair competition between and within industry sectors (McDowell).

McDowells' sentiments had been earlier advanced by former FCC Chairman Michael Powell who, in an address to the Senate Subcommittee on Commerce, Justice, and the Judiciary of the Committee on Appropriations, proclaimed that the FCC must undergo profound and dynamic change to keep pace with the unprecedented revolution in communications between and beyond the Communications Act of 1934 and the Telecommunications Act of 1996 which demanded a new FCC business model (Federal Communications Commission, 2001).

Chapter 9

Organizational Implications of Limiting FCC Merger Reviews

Using the directives of the Telecommunications Act, the FCC has engaged in more diligent review of telecommunications companies' merger proposals although the Act did not increase FCC merger authority (Troy, 2001). Indeed, no provision of the either the Communications Act or Telecommunications Act supports the commission's merger-review interest (Brenner, 2005). Moreover, Brenner views the FCC's obsession with reviewing corporate mergers contradictory to the deregulatory objectives of the Telecommunications Act (Brenner). While the FCC was given the authority to ascertain whether proposed license transfers and transfers of interstate operational authorizations to confirm that they are truly in the "public interest, convenience and necessity," the 1996 Telecommunications Act also grants the commission authority to impose conditions on transfers of licenses (Robbins, 2006). In addition, restraint of trade issues prohibiting conglomerations with restraint of trade implications are established under the dominion of the Federal Trade Commission as outlined in the Clayton Act (Robbin). However, the Commission has not justified any decisions using this new authorization because they must be justified upon strong evidentiary standards not required in establishing "public interest" arguments, which, by their very nature, invite questionable and inconsistent results (Troy).

The FCC has seemingly preferred to subject companies to covert pressure to accede to "voluntary" conditions rather than analyzing the merits of a proposed transaction pursuant to established rulemaking and adjudicatory procedures (Troy, 2001). This practice has invited companies seeking merger approval to unwittingly accept conditions instead of running the risk of costly delays or disapproval of merger proposals. Activities of this nature signal a discordant move from the FCC commitment to public participation promised by the Telecommunications Act. Further complicating matters is that FCC decisions have not provided any clear precedents that can be used by businesses as a template or guide which would aide them in assessing the predictability of any merger proposals (Toth, 1994).

The FCC's predisposition with expanding merger reviews into lengthy investigations of proposed merging parties business practices has been viewed as an invasive misuse of the public interest review responsibility (Duffy & May, 2005). Industry representatives argue that not only does the commission lack this authority, but it represents a duplication of responsibilities of the Federal Trade Commission and the Department of Justice's Antitrust Division (Duffy & May). In this light, the FCC's actions often serve the purpose of exacerbating the problem as it contributes to a perception of wasteful government resources and creates an atmosphere of apprehension resulting from the inconsistent decisions and opinions coming from the FCC.

The FCC's application of public interest standards to merger reviews fails to provide a reliable and consistent decision making platform and the FCC decision chronology has failed to establish a sound rationale for distinguishing between mergers that deserve intense analysis and those that should be subjected to the more limited review (Parkinson & Parkinson, 2006). The FCC's stated rationale suggests that mergers violate the public interest if they are determined to have "anti-competitive" yet broadcast industry proponents insist that this fails to provide a substantive standard that will result in approval or justify disapproval decisions (Nuechterlein & Weiser, 2005). As such, bro9adcast representatives feel that the FCC and the public interest are better served if merger decisions were restricted to a determination of whether a merger or license transfer would violate any existing federal laws or regulations instead of attempting to interpret violations of the "public interest" standards (Nuechterlein & Weiser).

According to Bauer and Wildman, economic theory suggests that the use of "voluntary" conditions should be discouraged unless there is a violation that such a compromise would directly mitigate (Bauer & Wildman, 2006). They suggest that it would be more appropriate for the FCC to apply uniform, transparent, and widely distributed standards for measuring the strength of a proposal to address the public interest. In the absence of such clear cut criterion, Bauer and Wildman fear that the process is fraught with land-mines and will work to the disadvantage of the FCC pursuit of the public interest protections under its limited power to review and condition license transfers (Bauer and Wildman).

Chapter 10

Forbearance: A Regulatory Enforcement Headache

The Communications Act of 1934 mandated that the FCC impose tariffs to assure reasonable rate. In many cases this tariff was passed on to customers although the 1996 Telecommunications Act attempted to provide some relief from this practice for nondominant interchange carriers so as to promote competition in the marketplace. For the most part FCC tariffs were upheld by the Supreme Court in cases brought by monopolistic service providers. FCC actions to change to a nontariff structure for upstart carriers (all other than AT&T) were not welcomed by the courts.

The passage of the Telecommunications Act of 1996 changed the approach and directed the FCC to

(a) forbear from applying any regulation or any provision of this chapter to a telecommunications carrier or telecommunications service, or class of telecommunications carriers or telecommunications services, in any or some of its or their geographic markets, if the Commission determines that—

(1) enforcement of such regulation or provision is not necessary to ensure that the charges, practices, classifications, or regulations by, for, or in connection with that telecommunications carrier or telecommunications service are just and reasonable and are not unjustly or unreasonably discriminatory;

(2) enforcement of such regulation or provision is not necessary for the protection of consumers; and

(3) forbearance from applying such provision or regulation is consistent with the public interest (FCC, 2007).

The Telecommunications Act in an effort to avoid any future "hang-over" provisions of the 1934 communications Act afforded the FCC with the luxury of choosing to selectively enforce or ignore at it's sole discretion any regulation or provision of the 1934 Communications Act, if the commission determines that:

1. Enforcement of such regulation . . . is not necessary to ensure that the charges, practices, classifications, or regulations . . . in connection with that telecommunications service are just and reasonable and are not unjustly or unreasonably discriminatory;

2. Enforcement of such regulation or provision is not necessary for the protection of consumers; and

3. Forbearance from applying such provision or regulation is consistent with the public interest (Troy, 2001).

This provision provided the FCC with a monumental trump card that many feel it has not exercised enough. Others view the FCC exercise of its newfound authority to be arbitrary and at cross-purposes with the mandate of the Telecommunications Act purpose of clarifying FCC positions. Although the statutes clearly place the responsibility for justifying any FCC reliance upon forbearance clauses squarely with the FCC, in many cases, the agency shifted responsibility for providing justifications to the petitioning party (Troy, 2001). Notwithstanding, many officials feel that this practice is appropriate when the forbearance action would plainly result in increased competition or enhanced communications services for consumers (Teal, 2007).

Despite the Congressional intent, the FCC has routinely denied forbearance for many new entries in the telecommunications environment although it has granted partial relaxation of the rules to AT&T in response to its partition (Troy, 2001). Inconsistencies in making exceptions for established vendors while denying the same to upstarts has provided fodder for criticism from the business community and Congress. The Benton foundation argues that the engagement of smaller carriers in the regulatory rulemaking process would yield a stronger and more easily enforced set of standards (Benton Foundation, 2007).

Ironically, the FCC specifically lobbied congress forbearance authority arguing that forbearance from regulating carriers and services would save resources, reduce paperwork, increase efficiency, and promote competition consistent with the National Performance Review objectives. However, the FCC utilization of its forbearance authority has failed to produce many of these benefits (Troy, 2001).

Chapter 11

Escaping the Content-Regulation Quagmire

From 1949 to 1987 under the auspices of the FCC Fairness Doctrine individual broadcast stations were required to devote a reasonable amount of time to matters of public importance and offer reasonable opportunities for opposing viewpoints on controversial issues to be heard. Although there has never been an FCC license removal due solely to a Fairness Doctrine violation, if a station were deemed to have been in non-compliance with the FCC interpretation of "fairness", the broadcaster could be subject to lose of licensure through revocation or nonrenewal. Hentoff argued that if this were to occur, the FCC would have assumed responsibility for policing the First Amendment which was counter to the legislative intentions (Hentoff, 2007). The Fairness Doctrine was promulgated in 1949 by the FCC in an effort to require broadcasters to afford reasonable opportunity for the discussion of conflicting views of public importance. But in 1987, the FCC discarded the rule because it felt it had proven ineffective in encouraging open discussion of controversial issues presumably due to the self-censoring actions by broadcasters that had actually served as a chilling effect (Aufderheide, 1990).

FCC officials and legislators were also apprehensive that the Fairness Doctrine also violated First Amendment free-speech principles because it could be argued that by requiring broadcasters to broadcast opinions and programs contrary to their desires, free-speech privileges had been improperly manipulated (Hentoff, 2007). From a journalistic and free press standpoint, government involvement into content and programming decisions was argued restrictive to journalistic freedom of broadcasters and the editorial prerogative of broadcast journalists (Napoli, 2001). Although the FCC had originally justified the Fairness Doctrine because of limited and scarce broadcast spectrums, the theory lost considerable strength with the emergence and the proliferation of broadcasting alternatives and increased public access (Parkinson & Parkinson, 2006). However, although prevailing arguments have upheld the notion that the Fairness Doctrine violated the constitutional provision for a free press, it has not guaranteed public access to the publicly owned airwaves in a similar fashion to that afforded to the print media and the motion-picture industry (Schwar, 1995). Yet another challenge that continues to reverberate around the Fairness Doctrine is that many broadcasters suggested that the Fairness Doctrine inhibited them from freely airing issue-oriented advertising and public-service announcements because of the implied obligation to provide opposing viewpoints (Aufderheide, 1990).

Although television remains a dominant purveyor of societal beliefs, attitudes, and practices, many regard it as a benign form of entertainment that needs constant regulatory oversight. The FCC has recognized this in its Annual Report to Congress:

Americans are voracious consumers of media services. On average, we spend close to 30 percent of our day engaged in some activity involving media, with television viewing the dominant media activity. For the September 2004-September 2005 television season, the average household tuned into TV for 8 hours, 11 minutes a day. This is almost 3 percent higher than the previous season, more than 12 percent higher than 10 years ago, and the highest level observed since television viewing was first measured by Nielsen Media Research in the 1950s. Within the same period, the average person watched 4 hours, 32 minutes each day, again a record high (Federal Communications Commission, 2006).

Thus a recurring policy obstacle is represented by the use of the First Amendment arguments against alleged "censorship" in television and radio programming. The National Association for Broadcasters argued that any requirement for specific programming to meet the needs of children was an "unconstitutional intrusion". Case law, however, suggests that the courts have upheld regulation of television and advertising content in a number of areas, including substances that are proven health hazards such as cigarettes and alcohol, and indecent programming. Broadcasters' right of free speech does not allow them to air cigarette commercials or programs in which the characters sit around and blow smoke at each other. In a frequently cited 1969 Supreme Court case, Red Lion Broadcasting Co. v. FCC (1969), the Court agreed that the FCC does not violate the First Amendment by concerning itself with television programming (Parkinson & Parkinson, 2006).

Unlike print media and the motion-picture industry, which are not regulated by the FCC and rely upon open-market competition for equilibrium, the broadcast airwaves are considered scarce natural resources despite arguments to the contrary that suggest that scarcity is overwhelmed by the proliferation of cable stations and other alternatives. In the absence of the Fairness Doctrine, another policy hot-point is related to determining exactly what obligation broadcasters must assume in exchange for the public licenses they receive. Broadcasters receive their license from the FCC. Supposedly, broadcasters receive a license in exchange for broadcasting in the public interest, which has been defined since 1960 to include children's television and the interests of young people (FCC, 1960). Broadcasters enjoy a "free and exclusive use of a valuable part of the public domain" (Charren, 1989). Timothy Worth, noted children's advocate, has questioned whether broadcasters can actually ever meet their public-interest obligation to children when "there is not one regularly scheduled weekday educational program offered by any of the major commercial television networks" (Children's Television Act, 1989). A remaining concern is the expectation in a number of lobbying arenas that the public's interest is best served when children receive special consideration and protection under the law, in a manner similar to that used in child labor laws, restrictions on purchasing alcohol and tobacco, seat belts and child-restraint laws, and child-abuse laws. In children's programming an important distinction between overall and specific programming exists. While many networks and advertisers argue that children's needs can be met through general family-oriented programming, which are essentially sex and violence free adult themed programs. Child-development experts assert that for television to satisfy educational and developmental needs of children, it must be specifically targeted to that audience. While the Children's Television Act continues to permit broadcasters to use general programming to meet their public obligation to children, children of all ages continue to watch late afternoon and primetime television. According to media research the prime television watching time for children audiences ranging in age between 3 and 11 is between 4:30 P.M. and 11:00 P.M. and not during conventional early morning dedicated children's programming (Nielsen Media Research, 1990).

The argument for or against regulation is being recast as a question of choice. Those in favor of regulations call for choice in children's programming, and those opposed call for choice to change a channel or to turn off the television set. The Bush administration argues that cable and satellite offerings extend parental choice for children, undercutting the scarcity-of-broadcast-frequencies argument upheld by the Supreme Court in 1969 as a rationale for content-based regulations.

Chapter 12

Indecency, Obscenity and Profanity: Deciding What's Fair to Air

In August of 2005, the FCC announced the hiring of an anti-pornography activist as an advisor for its Strategic Planning and Policy Analysis Office, which was charged to reinvigorate the agency's campaign against broadcast indecency and to bring pressure on the cable industry to pull back some of its more offensive programming (Shields, 2005). If the FCC sanctions a broadcaster it may deny future license renewals, issue monetary fines, or impose an immediate license revocation. During the Powell tenure, the commission stiffened its enforcement posture by imposing an incident based monetary penalty system that would assess a fee for each indecent utterance in a broadcast, rather than just imposing a single entire broadcast penalty. While Michael Powell favored a more open-content regulation, Kevin Martin favors heavier fines and quicker resolution of indecency complaints that had lingered for years (Shields). After Janet Jackson's "wardrobe malfunction" led to a bare bosom during the 2004 Super Bowl halftime telecast, Congress intervened to step up pressure on broadcasters through the FCC to route out sexual content (Vivian, 2006). Indecency concerns were ramped up due to Howard Sterns' all-out disregard of FCC complaints and his failure to pay subsequent fines; the NFL's airing of a promotional vignette in which a fully dressed player was greeted by a towel dropping woman in the locker room before a game; plans to broadcast the film "Saving Private Ryan" which opens with a foray of profanity on Veterans Day; Oprah's show devoted to teenage sex; and Don Imus' ridicule of a female basketball team, all became battlefronts pitting the networks against the FCC (Vivian). These concerns eventually drifted over to cable operators as the FCC repeatedly called on satellite and cable operators to devise family-friendly programming tiers and/or unbundled "a la carte" channel selection for customers under the threat of seeking to apply to pay TV the indecency strictures that must be met by broadcasters (Shields). Opponents to this approach led by Comcast and Time Warner argued that these approaches would raise retail cable rates and reduce programming diversity (Hearn, 2007).

Chapter 13

Ownership Rulings Crisscrossed

The FCC has withstood strong pressure to reform restrictions on ownership of multiple media outlets despite the incessant pressure from the broadcast industry and its supporters, although it has from time to time discussed plans to change the rule prohibiting ownership of both a newspaper and a broadcast outlet in the same market (Champlin & Knoedler, 2006). The Telecommunications Act recognized the advantages that flow from common ownership of media outlets in the same market and directed the FCC to repeal its cable-television cross-ownership rule and as well to modify several other ownership restrictions (Troy, 2001). The Telecommunications Act also required the FCC to conduct biennial reviews covering all of its regulations, including its ownership restrictions, to determine whether any required modification to support the public interest and competition objectives it purported (Champlin & Knoedler). After 2 years of deliberation, the commission issued its first Biennial Review Report for 1998 on June 20, 2000 which detailed significant increases in the number of media outlets participating in the public spectrums. Yet, the FCC's posture failed to acknowledge that the rapid introduction of media outlets had expanded the communications marketplace to an almost saturated level of competition at which would deem ownership restrictions of little value in assuring diversity in ownership and broadcast content. The FCC determined that the vast majority of the ownership rules on the books were supportive of public interest objectives and thus should remain unchanged (Potter, 2003).

Under former Chairman Michael Powell the FCC actually voted to repeal the cross-ownership rules that prevent a media company from owning both a television station and a newspaper in the same town, but the federal courts ruled that the FCC had not justified its case for any rule changes (Goldfarb, 2007). As part of its Telecommunications Act requirement for biennial reviews, the FCC reported that it had modified rules that

- prevent one broadcast network from owning another broadcast network;
- limit the number of local broadcast stations that any one broadcaster can own to serving 35% of the TV-viewing households;
- prohibit a company owning cable systems and network stations in the same community; and
- prohibit cross-ownership of TV stations and newspapers in the same city (Bracy & Toomey, 2003).

Actually, the FCC originally intended to modify five of its media-ownership rules which would ease restrictions on the ownership of multiple television stations nationally and in local markets, local market cross-media ownership, and tighten restrictions on the ownership of multiple radio stations in specific local markets, but implementation was blocked by an appellate court (Goldfarb, 2007). A PEW Research Center report indicated that among those familiar with the FCC there was a overwhelming negative opinion of it (PEW, 2003). According to industry tabulations, over 9,065 public comments were filed associated with broadcast-ownership rulemaking (Docket 02-277) and only 11 of these supported the FCC rule change (Bracy & Toomey, 2003). Robert McChesney, founder of Free Press, stated that many citizens were troubled by the lack of publicity and outreach associated with the proposed rule changes especially since the vast majority of citizens viewed the proposed changes as a threat to democratic process and welcomed the opportunity to signal the FCC that no longer would it get away with making critical policy decisions behind closed doors, without public comment; and this practice had come to an end (Goldfarb, 2007). Despite this public sentiment and prior to the court challenge, then Chairman Powell issued temporary waivers for many companies and grandfathered others to protect interest acquired through merger and acquisition that may have been found in violation of the prohibited practices. However, in response to the lack of public support and adverse rulings by the courts, the FCC under the leadership of current Chairman Kevin Martin commissioned 10 economic studies to assess the implications of the changes to the FCC long-standing policy. The studies were completed in October 2007 and public comments have been invited. It is anticipated that Martin will lead an effort to update the rules after the public comments are gathered before the end of 2007.

Chapter 14

Avoiding Net Neutrality invites De Facto FCC Internet Regulation

The FCC has regulatory jurisdiction over all telephone communications, although not specifically the internet. However, given the growing use of voice over internet protocol (VoIP) services, the FCC is considering developing rules concerning enforcement of rules allowing internet calls and which would allow investigators to tap and trace them (Cable News Network [CNN], 2004). The justification for FCC involvement is premised on its legislative prerogatives and the appearance that phone calls made via high-speed internet connections bypass the conventional phone networks and threaten the competitive balance assured by the Telecommunications Act of 1996 (CNN). The FCC's investigation of AOL's Instant Messenger service during the AOL/Time Warner merger review served as evidence of the FCC's growing interest in the full range of internet communications (Bauer & Wildman, 2006). The FCC already possess the authority to decide whether the internet is a "telecommunications service" and thus subject to all of the FCC's regulatory requirements, which could invite a resurgence of problems similar to those encountered in the monopoly phone-network negotiations related to open access and instant messaging platforms controlled by a small group of large companies.

According to Troy's report, it seemed that the FCC has little intention of regulating the internet as a telecommunications service since it has already determined that the provision of internet access does not always engage a telecommunications service (Troy, 2001). The FCC has recognized the "negative policy consequences" associated with imposing strict internet regulations that may restrict the innovation, openness, and competition that characterizes the internet. However, Congress has entertained several "net neutrality" proposals that would establish an Internet Bill of Rights and authorize the FCC to impose fines up to $500,000, although the FCC would not be allowed to promulgate "net neutrality" regulations to restrict broadband-access providers directly (Hearn, 2006).

Chapter 15

That FCC Sunset is a Mirage

There has been mounting dissonance with regard to the ability and appropriateness of the FCC to continue as the sole arbiter of communication policy. In response, two policy groups issued reports in 1995 calling for the outright elimination of the FCC—the Heritage Foundation and the Progress and Freedom Foundation (Gilroy & Smith, 2004). Both groups insisted that FCC efforts to advance the public interest in accord with established legislation had been woefully lacking in that it organizationally, structurally, and legislatively had not evolved from its 1934 roots although the telecommunications industry had grown at warp speed (Crews, 2006). The Heritage Foundation recommended sun-setting the FCC within a 5-year timetable, although the more aggressive Progress and Freedom Foundation advocated a 3-year transition period (Gilroy & Smith). The Progress and Freedom Foundation plan would create a new Office of Communications in the executive branch to oversee the reconstruction of the subsidy-laden universal service to a needs-based system; the privatization of spectrum allocation; and antitrust enforcement (Gilroy & Smith). This entity would primarily be concerned with consumer protection in a similar fashion to the Federal Trade Commission (Hearn, 2007).

Similarly, the Heritage Foundation plan assigned FCC functions to other entities with interconnection and access matters, with voluntary agreements and disputes settled in the courts; with the radio spectrum becoming the province of the private sector; and the states assuming responsibility for assuring universal service (Gilroy & Smith, 2004). Advocates of both of these proposals cite the potential for improved responsiveness, faster access, and support for the competitiveness that the rapid technological environment commands (Crews, 2006). As a more viable alternative, other critics of the FCC have recommended reduction of the number of FCC commissioners to three to minimize the prolonged debates and some have even recommended the creation of a "telecom czar" (Gilroy & Smith). While these proposals recommended innovative approaches to regulation, streamlining of agency procedures, and enhanced public participation, the likelihood of a gradual termination is not considered to be plausible even though similar agencies like the Civil Aeronautics Board and the Interstate Commerce Commission have met this fate (Troy, 2001).

Although the 1996 Telecommunications Act promoted deregulation, the FCC continued to implement hundreds of regulations that are considered to have outlived their usefulness (Troy, 2001). Adding to this administrative burden, the FCC originated an additional 146 rules that contributed to a 24% increase in its budget request over 5 years and an estimated annual additional expense to consumers of nearly $105 billion (Crews, 2006). Although Congress proposed abolishing several agencies in 1995, the implementation of the Telecommunications Act of 1996 served to entrench the FCC despite the apparent need for fewer regulations (Crews). Many felt the agency failed to exercise self-restraint in regulating developing technologies which has inhibited necessary carrier infrastructure development to further technological innovation. Contrary to the pro-competitive and deregulatory purposes of both Gore's "Reinventing Regulation" initiative and the 1996 Act, the FCC continued to expand its discretion and to adopt regulations that were considered by many in the broadcast industry and its supporters to discourage competition in the marketplace. Market failure is the fundamental justification for the FCC intervention rationale. Although market failures are contingent upon economic and consumer shifts, as Commissioner Furchtgott-Roth wryly put it, markets do not fail "as often or as systematically as one might believe in Washington." Indeed, the FCC's recent regulatory approach does more to impair competition, and ultimately innovation, than it does to promote either of these goals (Troy, 2001).

In August of 1999, former FCC Chairman William Kennard introduced, "A New Federal Communications Commission for the 21st Century", although it is considered to have missed a golden opportunity to advance the deregulatory objectives of the 1996 Act (Furchgott-Roth, 2006). The plan recognized the existence of "vigorous competition that will greatly reduce the need for direct regulation" within the next 5 years, but it did not articulate what the FCC's precise reaction would be (Troy, 2001). Later Kennard delivered a "Report Card" on implementation of his plan to Congress on March 21, 2000, highlighting the FCC's progress in becoming a one-stop digital shop for consumers and again asserting the reality of increase competition in the telecommunications marketplace. The former chairman reported deregulation in several areas, but the report card failed to recognize that, at the same time, the commission has resisted pressure to elimination numerous regulations that were not considered by the industry and political supporters necessary. In this regard, the initial FCC Biennial Review proceedings had run contradictory to the intended goals of deregulation. Even when directed to do so by Congress and the President, the Commission remained steadfast in its unwillingness to cut obsolete and inappropriate regulations. Moreover, although the Report Card stated that the FCC's work was far from done, it failed to articulate a meaningful process for true deregulation which signaled that the FCC had not been able to progressively implement the goals of the 1996 Telecommunications Act (Troy, 2001).

Chapter 16

Toward a More
Customer-Centric Organization

In 1993, Vice President Al Gore introduced the National Performance Review (NPR), known as the National Partnership for Reinventing Government. The NPR was intended to "create a government that works better, costs less, and gets results." The NPR put forward many objectives intended to improve the actual and perceived improvement of government operations including, recognizes citizens as customers of government and putting them first, reducing unnecessary paperwork and red tape by phasing out unnecessary regulation, and making government regulation more understandable to lay citizens (Stern, 1994). The businesslike concepts of customers' first and improved customer service were to be indoctrinated into all aspects of government undertakings, especially in establishing a customer-centric approach to governing. In response the FCC promised significant internal structural changes and the creation of two new bureaus—a Wireless Bureau, to address personal communication services and the International Bureau to mitigate satellite and treaty-related issues (Stern). At the same time, the NPR was being touted by the Whitehouse as the longest and most successful national-government reform effort in U.S. history (Troy, 2001)

Although FCC internal enhancements were a priority for then Chairman Reed Hundt, who also installed a series of customer-service standards, the commission was and is often criticized for woeful performance of fundamental business activities, including returning phone calls and emails, and for maintaining a huge backlog of applications, petitions, and legal challenges (Troy). In response the FCC sought to reassure that its customer's input weighed in commission deliberations so the organization, as a symbolic gesture, began holding regional meetings with public-interest groups to construct a dialogue (Heffron, 1983). Subsequent FCC leaders have also readily admittedly that the agency has been unsuccessful in implementing an effective customer-service culture throughout the organization and have routinely reported this as part of the Annual Performance Report to Congress (FCC, 2007).

Part III

Transformational Leadership, Strategic Planning & Outcome-Oriented Regulatory Practices

Chapter 17

The Perfect Storm—Inadvertent Convergence of Programs and Personnel

The communications landscape has changed tremendously over the past 10 years and the vast majority of the FCC's rules were enacted at a time prior to the almost universal internet and cellular utilization. Congress through the provisions of the Telecommunications Act accepted this reality and in response required the FCC to review its full slate of rules, regulations, and policy positions recognizing that the FCC has often either lacked the capacity or exhibited an unwillingness to make the changes in the communications marketplace. Not only has the FCC steadfastly refused to modify its content and ownership regulations, but in some cases the agency has increased regulatory burdens upon its stakeholders and unintentionally revived policies that it had previously declared constitutionally flawed (Troy, 2001). While it is often common practice in the FCC to "Do-Act-Check, then Do it again," a much more 'front-end loaded' strategic approach is favored by enlightened organizations. Information and diverse input drives good decision making and solid knowledge-based decisions are guided by the systems-resources approach (Tompkins, 2005). This is especially important for repetitive assignments and for those where accountabilities in the form of annual reporting, program evaluations, and budget justifications must be provided. This systematic process of goal achievement and continuous improvement has been a precursor to recent developments in quality-improvement programs and to counter the hastily contrived incremental inclination characteristic of the FCC in previous years (Tompkins). A more formidable and solid foundation is provided by Jurman's 'three-pegged stool' trilogy which offers a structural approach of quality planning, quality control, and quality improvement (Tompkins). This is even more important for the FCC where resources are scarce and demands from a cadre of stakeholders are intensifying.

This approach not only establishes clearer lines of communication, but also establishes a process that should result in a continuous improvement in communications with stakeholders throughout all units of the organization. A committed planning process ensures that strategies evolve from a sound and comprehensive conception of needs and responsibilities. Certainly, the FCC has been burdened by the need to satisfy the disparate demands made on it by multiple constituencies, yet it has been able to balance them in an apparently successful manner as prescribed by the social-constructionist school of thought (Toth, 1994). A sustained evaluation process will shed light on the potential for optimization in the delivery of these services and this has become the charge of its new Strategic Planning and Policy Evaluation unit (FCC, 2007). Especially with regard to external demands, strategic evaluation will assure that programs and activities are clearly and persuasively delivered in each service area; these can then be confirmed by using periodic surveys and focus groups followed by structured dialogue with both consumers and stakeholders.

Chapter 18

The Volatile Nature of the FCC's Performance Planning

The FCC has typically organized itself around groups of activities based on products, services, customers, and geography that helped to create different and often-conflicting regulatory frameworks independent of each other. This meant that there was little knowledge seepage between units as internal work was performed in one of several functional areas that operated as almost independent bureaus in addressing its stakeholders' transactions, monitoring, rule enforcement, and adjudications. This framework results in a highly technical staff of functional experts. If the FCC is to become more effective, as measured by increased problem solving and goal accomplishment, it must embrace the promise of deregulation internally and shun the independent-unit organizational structure it has favored since its inception.

The FCC leadership recognizes that the organization does not operate in an ideal world, and in response has managed to adapt by aimlessly continuing to get things done (Lindblom, 1959). But the caveats of "incrementalism" or "disjointed incrementalism" have to be taken into account along with the costs of a course of taking only marginal steps with minimal departure from the status-quo. Innovation and progress oftentimes demands large movement, forward thinking, and totally new approaches that will not be forthcoming in the FCC's incremental approach. Recognizing this Berry stated,

> managers have been moving away from traditional hierarchically managed agencies towards a management style that highlights responsiveness to citizens, excellent quality services, employee empowerment in the workplace, and an on-going strategic planning process . . . in a disciplined effort to produce fundamental decisions and actions that define what an organization is, what it does, and why it does it. (Berry, 1994)

Chapter 19

Brilliance Is Not Always Practical

The FCC must find a way to work across and between its independent units in a cross-bureau approach similar to the Wireless Access Task force. The FCC Strategic Plan suggests such a commitment as it includes a general goal of modernizing operations as one of its six identified foci for 2006-2011 (Federal Communications Commission, 2006). Both the FCC and Congress recognize the importance of a highly productive, adaptive, and innovative organization achieve the objectives of the 1996 Telecommunications Act to address many of the new technological challenges. The FCC Communication Plan clearly articulates this:

> The FCC's strategic planning process for 2006-2011 outlines a path that ensures that an orderly framework exists within which communications products and services can be quickly and reasonably provided to consumers and businesses. Equally important, the plan also addresses the communications aspects of public safety, health, and emergency operations; ensures the universal

availability of basic telecommunications service; makes communications services accessible to all people; and protects and informs consumers about their rights. (FCC, 2006)

The FCC has heeded this call recognizing that it cannot wait to receive the benefits that can be achieved only through true deregulation of the communications industry for fear that it will fall even further behind in its response to the rapidly converging technological landscape (Troy, 2001). Michael Powell as early as 2001 called for FCC reform that included a comprehensive retooling and redirection of the commission's entire mission. He advocated building a new business plan along four dimensions of (a) a clear policy vision that could be used to guide FCC deliberations (consistent with prevailing communications statutes and rules); (b) a stronger emphasis on building a strong management team given the tools to produce a cohesive and efficient operation leading to clear and timely decisions; (c) an extensive training and development program to build employee capability and to ensure that employees keep pace with the technical and economic trends; and (d) an organizational restructuring to align the FCC with the realities of the new marketplace (Energy Hearings, 2001).

Similarly, an elevated state is reserved for "rationalism" and the strategic-systems approach to policy and decision making—it should, according to Bryson and Roering, defined what an organization is, what it does, and why it does it (Bryson and Roering, 1988). Bryson and Roering went on to suggest that it is generally understood that most initiatives directed to produce fundamental change in government through strategic planning will fail, due to the inherent weaknesses of time, information availability, the pressures of public accountability, and the broad spectrum of participants it consumes as resources. This certainly reinforces the contention that the ultimate calling for this process is to only prescribe the ideal, recognizing that it can never actually be achieved.

Chapter 20

Transformation Can Be Rough Around the Edges

There appear to be many schools of thought on what it takes to be successful in implementing an effective strategic planning process. Bryson and Roering (1988) purported that a government must have a process sponsor, a process champion, a strategic planning team, openness to disruption, a high tolerance for time lapses, flexibility, the acceptance of milestones as progress, and an honest confidence in the evaluative criteria (Bryson & Roering, 1988). Alternatively, Wechsler and Backoff (1986), advanced the notion that types of strategic planning are warranted based on the strategic situation of the agency and the key to success is to match the right approach to the situation. The authors identified the different approaches as the transformational strategy, the protective strategy, and the political strategy, each with its own set of considerations (Wechsler & Backoff). Berry, on the other hand, identified four factors that explain why certain agencies pursue innovation through strategic-planning processes and surprisingly "peer pressure" and "keeping up with the Jones" ranked as the highest motivations for initiating strategic-planning processes. These were followed by changes in political administrations as they establish their agendas; the degree to which agencies do business with private-sector companies beholden to strategic planning; and threatened financial resources (Berry, 1994).

Even with these modifications, maintaining and sustaining a successful FCC strategic-planning process will be constantly challenged due to the precarious position it holds with regard to Congress and the President, competition for limited resources—financial, technological, and human—and public attention to its flaws. Further the pressures of accountability will exacerbate a huge toll on the process when the citizenry perceives that there are more immediate needs. Possibly the "mixed scanning" approach to decision making advanced by Etzioni (1995) provides a considerable alternative for immediate implementation for the FCC. Since it is neither rationalism nor incrementalism, it accommodates the need for as well as the inherent compatibility of both approaches. Scanning decisions and policy making are segmented and compartmentalized so that important strategic (contexting) decisions (who we are, what we do, why we do it) are made by exploring framed alternatives, which then provide the backdrop for operational (bit) decisions (Etzioni).

Larry D. Terry, in his article, "Administrative Leadership, Neo-managerialism, and the Public Management Movement," identified four public-management approaches—quantitative/analytic, political, liberation movement, and market-driven (Terry, 1999). He argued that "neo-managerialism" is nothing more than a more-sophisticated version of the managerialist ideology advanced to address the complexities and dynamism of our times and the challenges confronting today's public administrators (Terry, 1998). The FCC adoption of this new role requires that FCC managers be more active in the dialogue that determines the purposes of their organizations as well as the methods to be used to accomplish them. The new public-management philosophy is premised on managers taking more initiative and exercising leadership within and across the parochial parameters of their operational spheres. Although the neomanagerialism approach embodies a strong entrepreneurialism orientation which includes less bureaucracy, empowering employees, treating stakeholders as customers, and results-oriented missions, it would appear to be the perfect organizational foundation for the FCC's challenges. However, these approaches have historically run counter to the traditional leadership models that are built on a view of public service over self-interest orientation (Terry). Terry posited that the distrust of human nature and especially the self-interest, risk-taking, and rule breaking spirit of the public entrepreneur threatens democratic governance because it introduces public-choice theory, which suggests that humans are motivated by self-interest, deceitfulness, self-serving, and sloth, and are adept at exploiting others and, of course, should not be trusted. These characteristics intensify the need for greater accountability and protection of the public interest by the FCC.

Chapter 21

The Cold Business Calculus of Raising the Value of Information in a Competitive Environment

A recent Government Accountability Office study found that the FCC is fraught with leaks and has not taken proper safeguards to prevent or discourage sharing of confidential information regarding its coming actions with lobbyists (Dunbar, 2007). The report suggested that the agency tips off some people about what items are about to be voted, which in turn gives them an unfair lobbying advantage (GAO, 2007). The report says, "Situations where some, but not all, stakeholders know what the FCC is considering for an upcoming vote undermine the fairness and transparency of the process and constitute a violation of FCC rules" (GAO).

Although the FCC customarily shuts off all lobbying 1 week before any item comes before the commission for a vote, the GAO suggests that because the chairman of the FCC often decides which items are to be considered by the commission and circulates background on them at least 3 weeks before an upcoming meeting there is an invitation for impropriety that could easily have been closed by exercising leadership initiative (Behn, 1998). However, Behn suggested that initiative on behalf of public managers is not necessary to address the seven failures of governance—organizational, analytical, executive, legislative, political, civic, and judicial (Behn). Behn's argument is that governance is imperfect because human nature is imperfect and this is exactly why separation of powers and systems of checks and balances to protect against wrong doing go wrong. Behn also advances arguments against the entrepreneurial management paradigm, because of the reduced ability for monitoring and accountability (Behn).

Since the 1970s many government agencies have pursued a fully integrated, seamless decision-making process known as Strategic Planning & Management (Bryson, 1988). The rational model, accepting its human-nature imperfections and the influence of parochial politics, suggests that a succinct, calculated, and planned series of actions should lead to these utopian achievements. According to Graham T. Allison and Phillip Zelikow, "economics, political science, and to a large extent sociology and psychology study human behavior as a purposive, goal-oriented activity" (1999). As such, the strategic-management approach focuses on the nature of human choice and implementation in the public sector, aimed at achievement of a balance between purpose, present conditions, desired future outcomes, and inner and outer environments (Wechsler & Backoff, 1986)

Gulick's theory of administration stipulates that since every large-scale or complicated enterprise requires the efforts of many to carry it forward, all work, if it is to be the best work, must be divided and coordinated among workers to take full advantage of the unique knowledge, talents, and skills they bring to the task (Shafritz et al., 2005). Gulick identified three situations where such division should not occur—where work is less than full occupancy; the unit of work can not be further divided; and no advantage is gained by further dividing a task. Where these conditions are met in the FCC environment, the coordination of work is inescapable, according to Gulick, and it will be driven by structuring the organization or by the singleness of objective whereby individuals enthusiastically and on their own accord fit their skills into a unit. In these situations the whole is at its worst equal to the sum of its parts.

Chapter 22

Speak FCC Truth to Power through Outcome-Based Regulatory Processes

In the 21st century the reality of increasing competition for funds, attention, and patronage, a steadily growing cadre of often disconnected stakeholders with parallel, intersecting, and sometimes conflicting interests are increasingly imposing requirements on agencies like the FCC to provide solid evidence of their organizational efforts and the outcomes of their productivity in a unique combination of evaluation and accountability (Werther & Berman, 2001). Accordingly, Werther and Berman advanced the notion that effectiveness is essentially "doing the right things and efficiency suggests achieving their accomplishment in the right way" (Werther & Berman). In this accord, it may be interpreted that this multiplicity of interests has created a new logic of productivity in the context of evaluation and accountability in that the FCC must not only do the right things in the right way, but also at the right time, justifiably for the right reasons to be perceived to have satisfied obligations to all stakeholders. The ability to effectively and definitively assess and communicate the actual impact of FCC initiatives more than ever depends on strategic planning and programming, performance monitoring, evaluation, reporting, and public disclosure. Performance monitoring is a cybernetic process of collecting and analyzing data to measure the absolute and relative performance of a service, program, deliverable, process, or activity against expected results (Werther & Berman). To facilitate this, a defined set of performance indicators and measures must be constructed to regularly track on a monthly, quarterly, and semiannual frequency these key aspects of performance keyed directly to the goals and objectives of the FCC Strategic Plan as this will avoid any surprises that can undermine perceived organizational efficiency, effectiveness, and equity (Werther & Berman). On the other hand, the FCC should continue its practice of a structured, analytic effort undertaken annually to assess feasibility, appropriateness, and continued relevance of all its initiatives, programs and activities. Evaluation should be focused on matters of accountability and program improvement through a process of exploration, asking questions on why results are or are not being achieved; examining unintended consequences; debating issues and interpretations of effectiveness, relevance, equity, efficiency, and impact on long-term program sustainability in open forums, which may certainly co-opt internal and external antagonists (Stern, 1994).

Chapter 23

Back to the Future: Applying Sayre's Reality-Based Organizational Model to the FCC

Given the pantheon of organizational and leadership models in the context of the FCC operation, the Sayre Model appears to have hit the "reality" mark (Nikandrou & Eleni, 2003). Although there are some ambiguities surrounding the use and definition of the term *bureau*, Sayre's examples may diminish difficulties in actually distinguishing whether certain agencies, departments, or other organizational units qualify as bureaus and can be distinguished from the others that would not meet the criteria. This initial confusion seems purely an issue of semantics and possibly suffers from the language used at the time of the original writing. Sayre has defined the key operational entity in his model as the "bureau," as this has been described as an entity substantial enough to have power and authority necessary to make rules, prepare budgets, frame legislative proposals, and manage a complex personnel structure, which makes the sheer number of these power centers mammoth and possible overwhelming.

However, just by focusing on the role of the bureau chief, Sayre is able to isolate the key influencers on the policy, decision, and programmatic elements of the federal government (Held, 1979). In doing this, Sayre has identified the presidential, congressional, court, other bureaus, political party, media, interest group, and career staff as the major power and lines of influence in determining most federal decision making and as such these are the power lines affecting the FCC. His assertion is both significant and comprehensive. Interest groups and career staff should possibly appear higher on the list along with the media as an entity and a tool with its traditional and new technology trappings. They should be near the top of the hierarchy because most of the other lines of influence will be temporal and their weight will grow or diminish depending on the parochial issues at stake. The media's interests as participant, opinion shaper, watch-dog, and chronicler will be omnipresent and perpetual across all issues involving FCC operations, decisions, rulings, proposals, and staffing decisions. The recognition of the importance of the media is evidenced as most if not all agencies (bureaus) have equipped themselves with internal or external resources to manage media relations and the perceptions of their actions via community relations, intergovernmental relations, public relations, and other promotional activities. The media influence has also been known to circumvent "iron triangles" formed by congressional committees, interest groups and the bureaus themselves.

Sayre reinforces the dynamics of decision-making as a result of the interplay of these groups where each is seeking to exert influence on singular, multiple and continuous problem solving and policy matters. As such, the bureau chief must possess a combination of political skills, as well as a strong executive skill set (technical, administrative, managerial, human relations, and conceptual). After all, a bureau's effectiveness under the Sayre model is strongly hinged on it's ability to exercise what Sayre called the ABC's of politics—alliance building, bargaining, and compromise.

Sayre argued that his model is less a top-down model and more a bottom-up model as the actual expertise, tenure, and program history are normally held by career staff members and bureau chiefs than by political appointees, which is the experience at the FCC. Sayre also supported that the proliferation of duties across programs and jurisdictions has confirmed that there is no real separation of powers between the executive, legislative, and judicial branches but more a convergence of their cooperation (Landsbergen and Foley, 1996). Another interesting aspect of the Sayre model is the notion that it is a self-cleaning system that flushes out corruption and illegal activities. In this light, the FCC model already reflects the symbiosis of functions and authorities required for successful navigation of the tremendous conflicts of interests and technological advances. Similar to the manner in which Winston Churchill described democracy, the Sayre model is the worst model of how the FCC can work except[ing] all other models explored.

Chapter 24

Conclusion

Connecting Citizens to FCC Regulatory Outcomes—"Instituting a New Culture of Innovation and Accountability"

Each year the FCC promulgates many important rules through a process insulated from ordinary citizens proclaimed by the Administrative Procedure Act. Many observers believe that the internet can help bridge this vacuum and help to revolutionize rulemaking by allowing more citizens to participate in the development of government regulations (Coglianese, 2003). While the FCC actively solicits public comments to its proposals through the release of a Notice of Proposed Rulemaking and establishing a docket to gather information submitted by the public or the FCC pertaining to the proposed rule, the vast majority of this participation is done via traditional filings or email. However, more innovative technologies exist that may prompt more citizens—and particularly younger citizens—to participate in this valuable process, if this is indeed the goal. In the past few years many citizens have become increasingly more comfortable with and even dependent on tools that promote richer collaboration and networking including

YouTube, FaceBook, MySpace, Slashdot, and other online engagement-oriented communities; multiplayer multiple location on-line video games; wikis; information directories, and file-sharing software (Benjamin, 2006). These "e-tools" provide an opportunity to increase both the level and quality of citizen participation in rule-making, but may also offer quicker and a more reliable feedback on which an agency may act at significantly lower cost (Benjamin). Contrarians feel that, if successful, electronic participation may impose a significant nontrivial cost as agencies must devote resources to considering the new input (Coglianese, 2006). While the electronic citizen-participation approach could be used to assertively address and avoid future backlogs of unaddressed dockets that mire the FCC reputation, Congress and the courts may also benefit from such use (Benjamin).

Certainly, recognizing the many criticisms to an electronic citizen-participation process, it must be considered at a minimum an effective enhancement to the traditional methods of written comments, public hearings, and adjudication that have grown out of a sense that regular citizens have not been adequately heard or that they have been locked out of the process by institutional lobby groups (Furlong & Kerwin, 2005). As such, this approach appears to be an easily adaptable and easily implemented process that may yield considerable tangible and intangible benefits to the FCC in reestablishing the agency as responsive and innovative. This is particularly important given the multiplicity of stakeholders who often claim interests in the FCC's success and those who depend on it to protect the public interest.

References

Abernathy, K. Q. (2003). The role of the Federal Communications Commission on the path from the vast wasteland to the fertile plain. *Federal Communications Law Journal, 55*(3), 435-440.

Acumen PI—(2003), What are the factors contribute to make a good leader and how might your style of leadership change to be successful when involved in individual, racket and team activities., Date: 2003-04-14

Ahrens, F. (2005). *FCC indecency fines, 1970-2004.* Retrieved October 3, 2007, from http://www.washingtonpost.com/wp-srv/business/graphics

Allison, Graham T., & Zelikow, Phillip, (1999). *Essence of decision: Explaining the Cuban missile crisis.* New York: Addison-Wesley Longman.

Aufderheide, Patricia, (1990). After the fairness doctrine: Controversial broadcast programming and the public interest. *Journal of Communication, 40,* 48-72.

Aufderheide, Patricia, (1999). Communications policy and the public interest: The Telecommunications Act of 1996. New York, London: Guilford Press.

Aufderheide, Patricia, (2002), "Competition and commons: the public interest in and after the AOL-Time Warner merger", Journal of Broadcasting & Electronic Med, Dec 2002 Issue

Bauer, J., & Wildman, S. S. (2006). Looking backwards and looking forwards in contemplating the next rewrite of the Communications Act. *Federal Communications Law Journal, 58*(3) 415-438.

Behn, Robert D., (1998). What right do public managers have to lead. *Public Administration Review, 58*(3), 209-224.

Benjamin, Stuart Minor, (2006). Evaluating e-rulemaking: Public participation and political institutions. *Duke Law Journal, 55*, 893.

Benton Foundation. (2007). *Public interest obligations.* Retrieved October 20, 2007, from http://www.benton.org/issues/obligations

Berry, F. S. (1994). Innovation in public management: The adoption of strategic planning. *Public Administration Review, 54*(4), 322-330.

Block, Peter, (1993), Stewardship: Choosing Service Over Self Interest, Berret-Koehler Publishers, Inc., San Francisco, CA.

Bolden, R., Gosling, J., Marturano, A., & Dennison, P. (2003). *A review of leadership theory and competency frameworks.* Exeter, UK: Center for Leadership Studies.

Bracy, M., & Toomey, J. (2003). *Citizens urge FCC to retain current media ownership rules: Public records show overwhelming opposition to relaxing ownership caps.* Washington, DC: Future of Music Coalition.

Brenner, D. (2005). The 2005 Communications Act of unintended consequences. *Federal Communications Law Journal, 57*, 175-182.

Breyer, S. G., & Stewart, R. B. (1979). *Administrative Law and Regulatory Policy.* Boston: Little, Brown.

Bryson, J. M. (1988). *Strategic planning for public and nonprofit organizations: A guide to strengthening and sustaining organizational achievement.* San Francisco: Jossey-Bass.

Bryson, J. M., & Roering, W. D. (1988). Initiation of strategic planning by government. *Public Administration Review, 48,* 995-1004.

Burns, 1998.

Cable News Network. (2004). *Agency to regulate internet phone calls, Thursday, February 12, 2004.* Associated Press. Retrieved October 20, 2007, from http://www.cnn.com/2004/TECH/ptech/02/12/fcc.internet.ap/index.html

Cannon, Robert. "FCC 101: How to participate in FCC Regulation. (Government Activity)", Boardwatch Magazine, June 2000 Issue

Champlin, D. P., & Knoedler, J. T. (2006). The media, the news, and democracy: Revisiting the Dewey-Lippman debate. *Journal of Economic Issues, 40,* 135-152.

Charren, P. (1989, July). Testimony on the Children's Television Act. (Senate Hearing pp. 101-221). Washington, DC: U.S. Government Printing Office.

Children's Television Act, 104 Stat. § 996 (1990).

Children's Television Act. Hearings before the Senate Committee Television Violence and Children, 101st Cong., pp. 101-221 (1989) (Testimony of T. Wirth).

Coglianese, Cary, (2003), *The internet and public participation in rulemaking* (KSG Working Paper Series No. RWP04-044). Cambridge, MA: Kennedy School of Government.

Coglianese, Cary, (2006). Citizen participation in rulemaking: Past, present, and future, *Duke Law Journal, 55,* 943-968.

Compaine, B. (1984). Content, process, and format: A new framework for the media arena. In B. M. Compaine (Ed.), *Understanding new media, trends and issues in electronic distribution of information* (pp. 69-96). Cambridge, MA: Ballinger.

Crandall, Robert W. Sidak, J. Gregory Si, (2007), "Does video delivered over a telephone network require a cable franchise?", Federal Communications Law Journal, March 2007 Issue

Crane, J. S. (1983). Issues of the public interest regulation in supreme court decisions: 1927-1979. In J. J. Havick (Ed.), *Communications policy and the political process* (pp. 109-124). Westport, CT: Greenwood.

Crews, W. (2006, April 15). Sunset the FCC? *The Washington Times,* Retrieved September 10, 2007 from http://www. highbeam.com/doc/1G1-144546199.html.

Denhardt, R. B., Denhardt, J. V., & Aristigueta, M. P. (2002). *Managing human behavior in public & nonprofit organizations*. Thousand Oaks, CA: Sage.

de Figueiredo, John M. (2006), "E-rulemaking: bringing data to theory at the Federal Communications Commission.", Duke Law Journal, March 2006 Issue

Drucker, P. F. (1988). The coming of the new organization, *Harvard Business Review, 66*(1), 45-53.

Duffy, J. F. & May, R. J. (2005). *A digital age communications act: Report from the institutional reform working group.* Washington, DC: Progress & Freedom Foundation.

Dunbar, John, (2007), "Are all equal in FCC's eyes? GAO report says some parties get inside information.(BUSINESS)", The Houston Chronicle (Houston, TX), Oct 3 2007 Issue

Ellig, J. (2006). Costs and consequences of federal telecommunications regulations. *Federal Communications Law Journal, 58*(1), 37-102.

Etzioni, Amaita. (1995). *New communitarian thinking: Persons, virtues, institutions, and communities (constitutionalism and democracy)*. Charlottesville, VA: University of Virginia Press.

FCC Restructuring, *Hearings before the Senate Subcommittee on Commerce, Justice, State, and the Judiciary of the Committee on Appropriations,* 107th Cong., (2001) (Testimony of M. Powell), Retrieved on September 5, 2007 from http://www.fcc.gov/Speeches/Powell/Statements/2001/stmkp128.html

Federal Communications Commission, (1993), History of wire and broadcast communication.

Federal Communications Commission, (1999). *The public and broadcasting.* Washington DC: Mass Media Bureau.

Federal Communications Commission, (2001), New Beginnings, Summary Testimony of Chairman Michael Powell, Retrieved September 18, 2007 from http://www.fcc.gov/Speeches/Powell/Statements/2001/stmkp128.html

Federal Communications Commission, (2004). *Biennial Regulatory Review 2000, Staff Report, September 18, 2000.*

Federal Communications Commission, (2006), *Twelfth Annual Report,* Released March 3, 2006.

Federal Communications Commission. (2007a). *Commissioners from 1934 to Present.* Retrieved July18, 2007, from http://www.fcc.gov/commissioners/commish-list.html

Federal Communications Commission. (2007b). *Complaint and Enforcement Statistics.* Retrieved July18, 2007 from, http://www.fcc.gov/eb/oip/Stats.html

Federal Communications Commission. (2007c). *FDCH Congressional Testimony, March 14, 2007.*

Fiedler, F. E. (2005), The contingency model of leadership effectiveness: Its levels of analysis. *Leadership Quarterly, 6*(2), 147-167.

Fischer, R. L. (2002, January 1). *What lies ahead for the Federal Communications Commission? Under Chairman Michael Powell, the FCC will be pushing a conservative agenda concerning regulation and deregulation in telecommunications. USA Today, 130.*

Fowler, M., & Brenner, D. (1982). A marketplace approach to broadcast regulation. *Texas Law Review, 60*, 207-257.

Furchtgott-Roth, H. W. (2006). *A tough act to follow? The Telecommunications Act of 1996 and the separation of powers.* Washington, DC: American Enterprise Institute.

Furlong, S. R. (2005). Interest group participation in rule making: A decade of change. *Journal of Public Administration Research and Theory, 15*(3), 355-370.

Geller, Henry (2003). Promoting the public interest in the digital era. *Federal Communications Law Journal, 55*(3), 515-520.

Gilroy, A., & Smith, M. (2004). *The Federal Communications Commission: What role for the future?* Washington, DC: Congressional Research Service Report 96-535.

Goldfarb, Charles B. (2007), "FCC media ownership rules: current status and issues for Congress.(Federal Communications Commission", Congressional Research Service (CRS) Rep, March 2007 Issue

Gordon, J. A. (1994). Reviewing the national performance review: A critique of reinventing government. Cambridge, MA: Public Policy Journal, Kennedy School of Government, Harvard University.

Guttman-McCabe, Christopher Mushahwar, A., (2005), "Homeland security and wireless telecommunications: the continuing evolution of regulation", Federal Communications Law Journal, May 2005 Issue

Greppi, M., Halonen, D., & Lisotta, C. (2005). FCC's Powell at end of rocky road. *Television Week, 24*(4), 1-61.

Gutwein, P., II. (2000). The FCC and Section 312(a)(7) of the Communications Act of 1934: The development of the "unreasonable access" clause. *Federal Communications Journal, 53*(1), 176.

Haigh, R., Gerber, G., & Byrne, R. B. (1981). *Communications in the 21st century.* New York: Wiley.

Hausman, Jerry A. Sidak, J. Gregory, (1999), "A consumer-welfare approach to the mandatory unbundling of telecommunications networks.", Yale Law Journal, Dec 1999 Issue

Hearn, Ted, (2007), *TV Violence may Further Chill Frosty Relations with FCC's Martin*, Multichannel News retrieved September 10, 2007 from http://www.multichannel.com/article.

Heffron, F. (1983). The FCC and Broadcast Deregulation. In J. J. Havick (Ed.), *Communications policy and the political process* (pp. 39-70). Westport, CT: Greenwood.

Held, W. G. (1979). *Reconstructed: Decisonmaking in the federal government, the Wallace S. Sayre model.* Washington, DC: Brookings Institution.

Helein, Charles H. Marashlian, Jonathan, (2002), "Detariffing and the death of the filed tariff doctrine: deregulating in the "self" interest.", Federal Communications Law Journal, March 2002 Issue

Hentoff, N. (2007). Policing the first amendment. *Washington Times.* Retrieved August 30, 2007, from http://www.washingtontimes.com/

Hilliard, R. L. (1991). *The Federal Communication Commission: A primer.* Boston: Focal Press.

HRG.031407: Regulatory Philosophy, Statement Summary of Commissioner Robert M. McDowell, Federal Communications Commission before the Subcommittee on Telecommunications and the Internet Committee on Energy and Commerce, United States House of Representatives, retrieved from http://energycommerce.

house.gov/cmte_mtgs/110-ti-hrg.031407.McDowell-Testimony.pdf., August 14, 2007.

Katz, D., & Kahn, R. (1978). *The social psychology of industry.* New York: Wiley.

Landsbergen, David Orosz, Janet Foley, (1996), "Why public managers should not be afraid to enter the "gray zone": strategic management and public I", Administration & Society, August 1996 Issue

Lasar, Matthew, (2008), Interview: Laying it on the line with FCC chair Kevin Martin, http://arstechnica.com/features/2008/10/fcc-interview-kevin-martin/

Lasar, Matthew, (2008), http://arstechnica.com/uncategorized/2008/12/no-more-porn-filtering-on-fcc-free-wireless-broadband-plan/

Lasar, Matthew, (2008), http://arstechnica.com/uncategorized/2008/12/fccs-martin-and-white-house-feud-over-smut-free-broadband-plan/

Lehman, Dale and Weisman, Dennis, 2000, The Telecommunications Act of 1996: The "Costs" of managed Competition, Kluwer Academic Publishers, Norwell, MA.

Linker, J. (1983). Public interveners and the public airwaves: The effect of interest groups on FCC decisions. In J. J. Havick (Ed.), Communications policy and the political process (pp. 149-170). Westport, CT: Greenwood.

McChesney, Robert, and Schiller, Dan, (2002), The Political Economy of international communications: Foundations for the Emerging Global Debate over media ownership and Regulation, UNRISD world summit. Retrieved on September 5, 2007 from http://www.robertmcchesney.com/articles.html

McConnell, Bill, (2005), Kevin Martin's Challenge: New FCC Chairman could pose problem for Big Media, News & Comment, Broadcasting & Cable, March 21, 2005 Issue.

Messere, F. (2002). Regulation. In C. H. Sterling (Ed.), Encyclopedia of Radio. Chicago: Fitzroy Dearborn.

Moon, Myung Jae (1999), "The Pursuit of Managerial Entrepreneurship: Does Organization Matter?", Public Administration Review, Jan 1999 Issue

Mueller, Milton."Myth made law (1997), (Telecommunications Act of 1996)", Communications of the ACM, March 1997 Issue

Napoli, P. (2001). *Foundations of communication policy: Principles and process in the regulation of electronic media*. Creskill, NJ: Hampton Press.

Napoli, P. M. (2003). The public interest obligations initiative: Lost in the digital television shuffle. *Journal of Broadcasting & Electronic Media, 47*(1), 153-156.

Napoli, P. (2006). *Media diversity and localism, meaning and metrics*. Mahwah, NJ: Laurence Erlbaum.

Neuchterlein, Jonathan and Weiser, Philip, (2005), Digital Crossroads: American Telecommunications Policy in the Internet Age, MIT Press, Boston, MA.

Nielsen Media Research. (1990). *Report on television*. Northbrook, IL: Nielsen Company.

Nikandrou, Irene Apospori, Eleni Papalex (2003), "Cultural and leadership similarities and variations in the southern part of the European Union.(resu", Journal of Leadership & Organizational S, Winter 2003 Issue

Nixon, D. C. (2001). Appointment delay for vacancies on the Federal Communications Commission. *Public Administration Review, 61*(4), 483-492.

Parkinson, M. G., & Parkinson, L. M. (2006). *Law for advertising, broadcasting, journalism, and public relations*. Mahwah, NJ: Lawrence Erlbaum.

PEW Research Center. (2003). *Strong opposition to media cross-ownership emerges*. Washington DC: Author.

Potter, Deborah. (2003). The big get bigger: the FCC makes a misguided decision. *American Journal Review*, Volume 25, Retrieved October 2, 2007 from http://www.ajr.org/Article.asp?id=3098.

Radvanovsky, R. (2006). *Critical infrastructure: Homeland security and emergency preparedness.* Boca Raton, London, New York: Taylor & Francis.

Red Lion Broadcasting Co. v. FCC, 395 U.S. 367 (1969).

Reiter, Harvey, (2005), "The contrasting policies of the FCC and FERC regarding the importance of open transmission networks", Federal Communications Law Journal, March 2005 Issue

Rich, J. Steven, (2006), "Brand X and the Wireline Broadband Report and Order: the beginning of the end of the distinction bet", Federal Communications Law Journal, April 2006 Issue

Robbins, Jim, (2006), The 1996 Telecommunications Act. *Federal Communications Law Journal, 58,* 559-570.

Robbins, Jim, (2006), "The 1996 Telecommunications Act. (Telecommunications Act of 1996: Ten Years Later Symposium)", Federal Communications Law Journal, June 2006 Issue

Schejter, A. M. (1999). The fairness doctrine is dead and living in Israel. *Federal Communications Law Journal, 51,* 281-300.

Schwar, James L., (1995). In the spirit of the law: An ethical alternative to the fairness doctrine. *Journal of Mass Media Ethics*, Volume 10:10.2, Retrieved July 10, 2007 from http://www.jmme.org/.

Senge, P., & Kleiner, A. (Eds). (1999). The *dance of change: Mastering the twelve challenges to change in a learning organization.* New York: Doubleday.

Shapiro, Stuart, (2007), "An evaluation of the Bush administration reforms to the regulatory process.(George W. Bush)", Presidential Studies Quarterly, June 2007 Issue

Shafritz, J. M., Ott, J. S., & Jang, Y. S. (2005). *Classics of Organization Theory* (6th ed.). Belmont, CA. Thomson Wadsworth.

Shales, T. (2004, November 21). Michael Powell exposed! The FCC chairman has no clothes. *Washington Post*, 1.

Shields, T. (2005, August 8). FCC hires conservative indecency critic. *Mediaweek*, Retrieved October 3, 2007 from http://www.mediaweek.com/mw/news.

Spitzer, Robert, (1993), Media and Public Policy, Praeger Publishers, Westport, CT.

Sterling, Christopher and Kittross, Michael, (2002), Stay Tuned: A History of American Broadcasting, Lawrence Erlbaum Associates, New Jersey.

Stern, Christopher, (1994). *Reinventing government comes to FCC*. Farmington Hills, MI: Federal Communications Commission, Broadcasting and Cable, Gale Group Reed Business Information.

Sussman, G. (1997). *Communication, technology, and politics in the information age*. Thousands Oaks, CA: Sage.

Taylor, Robert and Rosenbach, William, (2001), Contemporary Issues in Leadership, Westview Press, Cambridge, MA.

Teal, K. M. (2007). *Qwest again pushes for forbearance: CLECS ask FCC for rules*. Retrieved October 20, 2007, from http://www.phoneplusmag.com/hotnews/79h2015500.html

Terry, Larry D., (1998), Administration leadership, neo-managerialism, and the public management movement. *Public Administration Review, 58*(3), 194-200.

Terry, Larry D., (1999), "From Greek Mythology to the Real World of the New Public Management and Democratic Governance (Terry", Public Administration Review, May 1999 Issue

Tompkins, J. (2005). *Organization theory and public management.* Belmont, CA: Thomson Wadsworth.

Toth, Victor. J. (1994). One hundred new things for the FCC to do. *Business Communications Review, 24*(3), Retrieved August 15, 2007 from http://findarticles.com/p/articles/mi_hb5084/is_199403/ai_n18467834.

Troy, Daniel E. "Advice to the new president on the FCC and communications policy.", Harvard Journal of Law & Public Policy, Spring 2001 Issue

U.S. Government Accounting Office, 2007. GAO-07-1046.

Vivian, J. (2006). *The media of mass communication.* Boston: Allyn & Bacon.

Wechsler, B., & Backoff, R. W. (1986). Policy making and administration in state agencies: Strategic management approaches. *Public Administration Review, 46*(4), 321-327.

Weinberg, S. (1983). The politics of rewriting the Federal Communications Act. In J. J. Havick (Ed.), *Communications policy and the political process* (pp. 71-87). Westport, CT: Greenwood.

Werther, W. B., & Berman, E. M. (2001). *Third sector management: The art of managing nonprofit organizations.* Washington, DC: Georgetown University Press.

Wilson, K. (2000). *Deregulating telecommunications: U.S. and Canadian telecommunications 1840-1997.* Boulder, New York, Oxford: Rownam & Littlefield.